THE IRONWORKS

Sharpening Friendships and
Forging a Spirit of Vibrant Love

CALEB POPELKA

The Ironworks
Sharpening Friendships and Forging a Spirit of Vibrant Love

All Scripture quotations, unless otherwise indicated, are taken from
the Holy Bible, New International Version®, NIV®. Copyright
©1973, 1978, 1984, 2011 by Biblica, Inc.™ Used by permission of
Zondervan. All rights reserved worldwide. www.zondervan.com.
The "NIV" and "New International Version" are trademarks
registered in the United States Patent and Trademark Office by
Biblica, Inc.™

Scripture quotations marked (NLT) are taken from the Holy Bible,
New Living Translation, copyright ©1996, 2004, 2015 by Tyndale
House Foundation. Used by permission of Tyndale House
Publishers, Inc., Carol Stream, Illinois 60188. All rights reserved.

ISBN-13: 978-0-692-18175-1

Editing by Elizabeth Finkenbinder.
Back cover portrait image by Emma Reaves Photography.

Contents

PROLOGUE

Friendship is rewarding, heart-wrenching, enjoyable, difficult, joyful, sorrowful, frustrating, and life-giving all at the same time. Some friendships can't be defined; there are too many stories, laughs, and experiences to put a label on it. Some people have many friends and some have few friends. Friendships can be surface level acquaintances, or they can be rich with life. Most friendships are like a rollercoaster; there are twists, turns, ups, downs, barrel-rolls, and loops that can make your head spin.

But what does it truly mean to be a friend? What components make a friendship work? How do we be good friends to those that mean the most to us?

The truth is, there's no real set-in-stone answer to these questions. Friendships are messy and sometimes overwhelming. But they are also full of life, love, and reward for those who truly commit to another.

Although we can't be perfect friends, there are traits that we can embody that provide us access to a life full of unconditional love and lasting, meaningful friendships. These traits provide a framework for what it means to be a friend. They provide a foundation to stand on when times are flourishing with joy or drowning in hardship.

To discover what these characteristics are and how to embody them, we look to a man named Jesus. He is the perfect example of what a friend should look like. Every action, every word, every fiber of his being was made to sharpen us.

One of my favorite verses speaks of this very thing. It's so simple, yet so powerful in guiding us toward being the model friend. It's about a mutual, unspoken agreement to sharpen one another and point each other towards Jesus.

The New International Version puts it like this: "As iron sharpens iron, so one person sharpens another." The New Living Translation says it this way: "As iron sharpens iron, so a friend sharpens a friend." The verse is Proverbs 27:17, and I try to base my whole life around it.

I'm by no means perfect at living out this verse. Far from it, actually. But with these words in mind, we have the choice to be in a constant state of building one another up. We can sharpen each other so that we will be ready for any obstacle that comes hurling our way.

Iron, by mass, is the most common element on Earth. It forms the majority of Earth's inner and outer core. Iron is also vital to survival; without it, the body wouldn't be able to transport oxygen. It has been used in many tools in ancient history and is still commonly used today.

In the same way that iron is core to the Earth, friendship is a core element of our lives. Friendship keeps us from being lonely, gives us a shoulder to lean on, and sets us up for an adventure of a lifetime. There are a lot of people in the Earth, many who are desperate to be sharpened. Many of those people could be the people we know the best. So how exactly are we supposed to sharpen each other? How do we live by enhancing and loving each other in a way that transforms lives?

Like any person on Earth, I have many stories to tell. The stories in the pages to follow are about some of my friends, a few who will appear multiple times. These people I have grown to call "friend" embody characteristics that Jesus showed during his time on Earth and still shows to us today. I hope that by seeing some of these characteristics, we will have a clearer understanding of what it means to be a friend in the way Jesus is a friend to us.

Leave iron out too long, and it will begin to rust and tarnish. It will become frail and difficult to use again. Let's not leave each other out to rust. Let's sharpen each other, transform one another, and embody the traits of Jesus that make our friendships rich, strong, and durable – The Ironworks.

Chapter 1

RACQUET BUMPS

One of my favorite sports to play is tennis. I love the energy and focus that's required for the game. You have to exert quick bursts of energy to move to the ball, maintain focus on ball location and placement, and anticipate the next move of your opponent. It's also a mental game; you can't let one mistake define the game or everything will go downhill.

I especially love doubles. Having a teammate means that it's not all on you; you get to share some of the pressure. I love playing doubles at the net, mainly because smashing the ball is so fun. Plus, playing with a friend and sharing the passion for the game is all the more exhilarating.

I got to share this exhilarating experience with one of my best friends - Garrett. Throughout high school, we played on the tennis team together, but it wasn't until our senior year that we actually played doubles together. Every day we got out of class earlier than everyone else, so we would head to the tennis courts to practice.

One day we were hitting back and forth, and we decided we needed to come up with a secret system to outsmart our opponents. We were doing fairly well in games, but by coming up with a plan to communicate with each other while confusing our opponents, we thought we could put a few more wins on the board. The plan to outsmart our opponents was based on our movement around the court. If someone said "Texas", that was code for us to both run up to the net. If someone said "Cali", that was code for both of us to move horizontally across the court. "Cali" ended up being the most popular code word because whoever was at the net could quickly run across and smash the ball back and secure us a point.

We tried this system against other doubles teams at our school, and it ended up working well. In practice, we won every game we played using this system. We were practically set for the rest of the season. We had the perfect plan (or so we thought). We communicated well, and we were excited to play our first real match using this system.

However, the most satisfying and rewarding thing about playing tennis with Garrett wasn't our clever system. And it wasn't getting wins from our system either. It was the fact that after every point won or lost, Garrett would give me a racquet bump. A racquet bump is a tennis player's way of giving a high five without using their hands. In fact, I can't remember one single point where he didn't give me a racquet bump. It's kind of funny, I think there are more pictures taken of us giving racquet bumps than action shots.

In our first match using our coded communication system, it worked like a charm. We would confuse our opponents and be able to direct each other's movement to score easy points. Garrett would shout, "Texas," and I would run up to the net so the ball wouldn't get past us. I would shout "Cali," and he would run across the court for a Garrettesque slam. Slam after slam, point after point, success after success, and win after win. We were feeling great about our performance, and all the while he gave me a racquet bump after every point. It's easy to give racquet bumps when you're playing well.

But our system didn't always work. It was finally our time to shine at our district tournament. Our minds were racing with the thought of advancing to regionals and the mere possibility of even making it to the state tournament. Our blood was pumping full of excitement and hype for the upcoming matches. The first few matches at the tournament, we lived up to the hype. We won against every team and advanced in the bracket, all while racquet-bumping after every point.

The afternoon was filled with even more nerves and excitement than in the morning. We knew we still had a long day ahead of us, but we were confident that we could get the job done. So in our next match, we did what we knew how to do. We used our system like we always had. But something was off. Our opponents seemed to be figuring us and our system out. Every time we made a call, they would hit it in exactly the right spot away from us. Our system was not working the way it had been. We ended up losing that match, but the racquet bumps continued from Garrett despite all of the losing points.

Although we lost, we weren't out yet. There was still a chance we could advance to the regional tournament if we won the rest of our matches. There was still a sliver of hope that kept our enthusiasm alive. A few hours later, we began our next contest. It was a great game; it came down to the last set. The match was full of passion and emotion as we were determined to advance. So passionate in fact, that during the match that during our "Texas" call, Garrett took a wild swing and straight up hit me in the back of the head. It was painful, but guess what? Garrett still offered me a racquet bump even after the racquet bump to the head. We ended up losing that match, and our season was over. But what wasn't over was the encouragement, and he even ended up getting a scholarship from university officials who drove to witness his outstanding character.

What Garrett showed me is that a friend is there to encourage you through the good and the bad. We had great successes, and he gave me racquet bumps. Our system failed miserably, and he still gave me racquet bumps. Through every game, no matter how wildly exciting, triumphantly victorious, or heartbreaking the loss, Garrett was constant in the way he encouraged and lifted me up after every point. He showed me that after every point was a new chance. It didn't matter what happened in the last point, but it mattered that we had the opportunity to work together to make the next point go our way.

Jesus is like that, too. He's there for us in every situation no matter how good or how bad it is. In your greatest moments, Jesus is sharing the joy with you. In your darkest and most difficult trials, he's beside you telling you that you are worthy. No matter what you've done in the past and what yesterday held, he is constantly giving us new chances. Even if your system or plan didn't work out the way you intended, he makes all things new.

Jesus tells us that when we're enjoying our successes, life is going our way, and we're in the good waters of life, he will be with us. He tells us that when we face demanding trials, when life is beating us down, and we're face-to-face with a mighty river, the river will not overcome or sweep over us. He tells us that when we're in excruciating pain, when the grief of life is crushing us, and when we walk through the fire that will surely burn us alive, we will not be set ablaze.

Imagine if Garrett hadn't encouraged me after every point, especially during the games we struggled in. My confidence would have driven itself into the ground, and I probably would have performed even worse. I might have become upset at the fact that we were losing, which in turn might have caused me to take my frustrations out on him. It wasn't his fault that we were struggling, but I could have easily accused him of being in the wrong. I would have been left in the open to rust.

Instead, Garrett chose to embody the spirit of encouragement. By encouraging me through thick and thin, I was able to keep my head up and keep going. We were able to be a team because he understood the importance of lifting each other up. He understood that in order for us to have our best chance at winning, we had to forgive and forget each other's mistakes. We had to move forward, confiding and believing in each other's abilities.

Jesus will never stop encouraging you. He will always lift you up through thick and thin. He forgives and forgets, too. He wants to confide in you and you in him. He believes in you and your abilities whether you believe in yourself or not. He doesn't want to give you the best chance at winning. Why? Because he has already won.

There will be times in your life when you succeed, you are victorious, and you feel like nothing could ever possibly stand in your way. There will also be times when you fail and your plan doesn't go your way. The same is true of your friends. Your friends might also let you down and disappoint you. It's easy to become angry and start pointing fingers, but you have to forgive and forget. Jesus won the battle; he won the match against our failures. And he's forgiven all our mistakes. What would happen if we started forgiving like Jesus has forgiven us?

Encouragement is one of the best tools we have at our disposal to sharpen one another. It feels good to be encouraged, to be noticed, and to be believed in. It's the fuel that keeps the engine running on a cold, dark night. Words are powerful. If you say the right ones, it can transform entire lives just because you believed in them and spoke it into existence. Encouragement can light up eyes, hearts, and the lives of people you thought didn't have a spark left in them. Encourage people through everything, not just the easy moments. Sharpen, sharpen, sharpen the iron.

Chapter 2
A YEAR ON A MOUNTAIN

I'm the kind of person who loves a great adventure. If you have something to do outdoors, I'm there. Whether it's camping, hiking, kayaking, paddleboarding, climbing – you name it, and you've got me hooked. So when spring break of my junior year in college approached, the only thing to do was go somewhere that I've never been before. I love exploring new places and seeing the beauty of the untamed wild, so naturally I wanted to add a new destination to the list.

Along with my buddies, Garrett and Austin, we started to debate our travel destination well in advance of spring break. We dreamed of going to places far from home. But for my college bank account, going to a distant land was not so attainable. So we decided to embark on a backpacking journey to Guadalupe Mountains National Park. It was still a pretty good distance away from where I was – about an 8 hour drive – but nevertheless close enough and affordable enough for a college-ready adventure!

To divide up the travel time, Austin and I decided to drive to Garrett in Lubbock, Texas the day before our planned expedition. Before leaving, Austin and I needed to pack for the hike. I headed to his house, and we got two of his dad's old military backpacks to stuff with our necessities. Austin had never backpacked before, so we were both excited to see how it would turn out. Once we were all packed, we loaded up the car and were on our way to Lubbock.

The night before we left for the Guadalupe Mountains, we made a checklist of all the things we needed to bring and ensured that everything we mentioned was indeed in our backpacks. Early in the morning, we threw everything in the back of Garrett's car and began our journey to conquer the Guadalupe Mountains. Three friends, the outdoors, and no distractions. What could be better?

When we finally arrived, we were taken aback by the sight. Sure, they were no Rocky Mountains. But for Texas, this was a backpacker's paradise. After going through the necessary paperwork in the front office, we slung our backpacks over our shoulders and looked up at the mountain we were about to overcome. It was a nice, sunny day and not too hot - perfect weather for a backpacking hike. Before the ascent, we snapped a few pictures of us with our backpacks on and then headed to the trail entrance.

Upon arriving at the trail entrance, there was a park ranger who stopped us to check that we had our backpacking permit. Garrett retrieved the pass from his backpack and showed him that we had it. However, it seemed that the permit wasn't enough for this ranger. He seemed extremely skeptical of us and began asking us numerous questions.

"How long are y'all staying up there?" he asked.

"Not too long, sir, just two nights," Garrett responded.

"Two nights? Looks like a lot of stuff in your backpacks for two nights."

"Yes, sir, we came prepared," I said.

"What all do you have in there?"

And at that moment he was radioed in from another park ranger instructing him there was an emergency situation he needed to respond to. I don't know if he thought we were planning some sort of military operation on the peak because of our backpacks, but after that radio message, he just walked away. We were left feeling confused because he never gave us a clear go-ahead, but we weren't about to wait for him to return just so we could empty our whole backpacks only to have to repack them again. So we quickly moved on and started walking the trail.

The first night, we planned to camp out at Bush Mountain. The second night, we planned to spend at the highest point in Texas – Guadalupe Peak. For the trek to Bush Mountain, we needed to take the Tejas trail, a trail Garrett had apparently taken before. As we started on Tejas trail, I noticed it felt a lot hotter than it actually was. I checked the weather before we planned to make this hike, and it was supposed to be in the mid-seventies with a slight chance of rain during the first night. However, we weren't even thirty minutes into the hike, and I started to sweat. The backpacks were heavy, and frankly, I hadn't exercised in a while.

We took short, frequent breaks on the way up to rejuvenate and kept trekking. The way up was monotonous. It was twist after turn after twist after turn with no end in sight. Finally, after about two hours, Garrett pointed up and told us where the halfway point was. That's where we would stop and take a longer break and eat lunch. This, not surprisingly, became to be known as "Our Break Spot". Side note: Our Break Spot was not the halfway point at all. Either that was a lapse in Garrett's memory, or he was just trying to give us hope that there was a finish line. As we made our final push, I noticed some darker clouds moving in toward us from the other side of the mountain, but it didn't look like anything serious. Finally, we sat down at Our Break Spot and let out long groans of relief as we slid off our packs and took out our snacks. An energy bar never tasted so good.

After savoring what precious moments of rest we could, it was time to hit the trail again. At this point, the clouds that were moving in started to look a little more threatening. As soon as we went around the loop to the other side of the mountain, a blast of wind and cold air hit us. It was eerie the way the weather suddenly changed. A sudden temperature drop made it seem like something bad was bound to happen. As we started tackling the cutbacks again, the clouds caused me to become concerned. I told Garrett and Austin that we should try and pick up the pace to set up camp as the darkening clouds didn't look promising.

After another hour, our fears set in as we walked along an alarmingly narrow trail next to a ledge. The winds were relentless, and I'll be the first to tell you that when you have your body being pushed around next to a drop-off, it's not the best feeling in the world. We slowed down as we struggled against the incline and the unforgiving winds, and my legs virtually lost their function. No, seriously. They were cramping, I was in pain, and I could barely get them to keep me going.

We decided to take a break, and I was ready to call it a day, collapse, and sleep right where I was at. Garrett pulled out the map and gave us inspiring news: The campsite was only a mile and a half away! To our dismay, the mile and a half took us exponentially longer than we anticipated because it was full of constant elevation changes. Austin would humorously scream every time we encountered another hump. That mile and a half that we thought would take us an hour, maximum, took us double that. For two more hours, we desperately hoped we would finally reach the campsite.

Then, we found the Promised Land. When we saw the sign that said "Bush Mountain Campsite" with that majestic arrow pointing in the direction of bliss, we literally ran down the rest of the trail with our forty pound backpacks. We finally made it. We quickly unpacked our backpacks and set up two tents – one for us to sleep in, and one for our supplies.

Even though we secured the tent with stakes, even our supplies weren't enough to hold down the tent against the wind, so we had to throw a few stray rocks in with our backpacks. After successfully setting up camp, we enjoyed peanut butter and jelly tortilla wraps and watched a jaw-dropping sunset.

After the magnificent sunset, darkness crept its way through the trees, and the wind was still blowing steadily. We made our way into the tent and curled up on our sleeping bags to rest. We talked for a while, and then we heard the whistling of the wind through the trees. It didn't sound too extreme until thirty minutes later when it hammered our tent. I thought we were in the middle of a hurricane. On top of a mountain. This wind was terrifying! It could make grown men cry. It even picked up our tent at one point. No, I am not exaggerating. This wind lifted a tent with THREE college students laying inside.

Garrett said to me, "Caleb, I'm scared," and laughed nervously.

And I said, "I think I want to go back. We're going to die."

We tried to sleep through it but to no avail. The wind would hammer the side of the tent, pushing the tent fabric against my side. Simply the sound of the wind struck fear into my bones. There was no way I was getting sleep. Austin was the first to fall asleep, and I don't know how he even slept through the madness. Meanwhile, while Austin was sleeping, Garrett and I were busy being crybabies. This went on for hours, and then finally it let up enough to where I could fall asleep. I would wake up every so often to the wind still blowing, and then at one point it stopped as a small drizzle of rain fell on us.

When I woke up to the soft morning light shining through the tent, I thought I had died and gone to heaven. We had survived the brutal night. After that beating, we were ready to go and get back down off the wicked Bush Mountain. We got out of the tent, put on jackets, and packed up as quickly as we could.

As I was stuffing items back into my pack I hear, "Wait, is that…"

"Is it snowing?" I asked in disbelief.

Yep, it sure was. As if the weather could get any wilder, it started snowing. Wasn't it just 75 degrees yesterday? This wasn't even in the forecast. Honestly, it was magical. I felt like it was a reward for us braving the night. It snowed the whole time we descended, and we shared a few laughs over that park ranger who was so skeptical and intrigued by us having so many supplies in our backpack. It turned out we needed everything we packed for the hot and the cold, and we were proud of coming prepared. Take that, park ranger.

Our descent to the base took about half the time it did to ascend, and we stopped at Our Break Spot to take in the astonishing, snowy view. When we got back to the car, we threw our backpacks in the back and piled in to warm up.

Our appetite was never greater than in that moment. We consumed more fruit snacks, energy bars, and ham than is ever acceptable. Having full stomachs and content hearts, it was time to decide when we were going to make it up to our next destination – Guadalupe Peak.

We took one look at the rain that was starting to fall on the peak, and that pretty much decided it for us. Our legs were noodles, and we had just been through the most dramatic weather events known to man. It felt like we were up there for a year on that mountain; it felt as if we went through all four seasons and every weather event possible, so we didn't want to risk it again. Although it would have been cool to spend a night at the highest point in Texas, we ended up going home early. Maybe one day we'll go back and spend another year on that mountain, but for now, one was plenty.

That was no doubt a hard hike, but the journey was absolutely worth it. I wouldn't change a single thing. Austin and Garrett were troopers. For Austin's first backpacking trip, that probably traumatized him, but it will make all the other ones a piece of cake. What was so great about that trip is that we seemingly encountered it all and survived together. Austin came equipped with everything he thought we needed to survive, and it played out perfectly for us. We stuck together despite our fears, and there were little moments of victory that made the hike all the more worth it. Austin and Garrett are destined for adventure – it runs deep in their blood. And that adventure was full of surprises that tell an incredible story.

Jesus invites us on an adventure with him. The adventure is full of surprises and changing seasons. We'll go through spring, summer, fall, and winter. We'll go through joy, sorrow, comfort, and pain. But the adventure is worth it. The amazing thing about the adventure he invites us on is that we get more than just seasons. We get more than spring, summer, fall, and winter. We get more than joy, sorrow, comfort, and pain. We get more than just a year on a mountain. We get an eternity with him! An eternity of everlasting, fierce, and unconditional love.

There may be things in your life that look like a giant mountain you have to climb, and it may be taking you forever to get to your destination. You may have fears that are keeping you contained and winds that blow you in every direction. But Jesus is the ultimate mountain guide and the ultimate expert on impossible and exhausting hikes. With him, we don't have to be fearful because we know we'll survive the night. He will climb that mountain with you, help you step over every stone, and even carry your forty pound burden of a backpack. If he really wanted to, he could move that mountain right out of the way.

When we climb the mountains in our lives with Jesus, it provides us a spectacular view. We get to see where we came from, how far he's taken us, and take a deep breath of the fresh air as we enjoy seeing his beauty all around us. He's there in the big moments, like when we watched the sunset on top of the peak of Bush Mountain. But he's also there in the small moments, like when we witnessed the quiet snowfall of the morning. And he's even there protecting you from the mighty winds that try and blow you off the mountain. When we accept the invitation to his adventure, we get to go along on a journey that we know will be completely and undeniably worth it.

Friends need you to be there for them when they have to climb a mountain in their lives. They need you to be there through all seasons. Those seasons might be trying on you, and you might find yourself wanting to turn back and quit. But think about if Garrett and I had turned around and left Austin to conquer that mountain on his own. It was his first attempt at backpacking, and with all the crazy weather and our need to stick together, he probably would've turned back. I know I would have if I was alone. Either that or he would have never wanted to go backpacking again.

Jesus will never turn back or quit on you. Never. Just like he never quits on us, there should never be a time when you quit on your friends. Join the adventure with them and share the moments of victory together when you accomplish your dreams. Laugh together, conquer together, be scared together, and adventure together. Friends are adventurous. An adventure doesn't have to mean you go on an intense backpacking trip, but it does mean enjoying the seasons of life and conquering obstacles side by side. Sharpen each

other with adventure and know that the view at the top will
be worth the struggle.

Chapter 3
TIDE POOL

California: The Golden State. The land of Disneyland,
The Golden Gate Bridge, Hollywood, Yosemite National
Park, the Sierra Nevada, and some pretty rad beaches. I feel
like at one point in everyone's lives, they at least have
thought of going to California. From going to Los Angeles
and feeling like a celebrity (or maybe meeting one), seeing
the mountain ranges, swimming in the ocean, seeing the
sequoia trees, and so much more – what's not to like? That's
why when my calculus teacher invited me to go, there wasn't
a second of hesitation in me to accept the offer.

Jake was my calculus teacher from when I was in high
school. Now I think of him as a friend, and he has had a
profound impact on my life. Jake didn't just teach calculus;
he taught how to do life. His classroom was full of calculus
for sure, but it was also full of inspiration, life-lessons, and
thought-provoking discussions about the way the world
works. I always thought that Jake should be a life coach
rather than a calculus teacher and, ironically, now he is.
Every other year, Jake, along with his father, would take
students backpacking in the Sierra Nevada Mountains. They

called it the Sierra Challenge. Thankfully, I was chosen to go along with a few other friends.

Before we began the Sierra Challenge, Jake planned to take us all to Manhattan Beach to enjoy the sun and teach us how to surf. On one of those days, he took us to a tide pool. The plan was to explore the area, and there was a spot that you could cliff jump into a cove on the other side of the tide pool. We all hopped in the van and headed to the spot where we would spend part of the day. I don't remember who brought it or exactly why it was brought, but there was green face paint readily available to make us look like warriors. We looked fierce (and probably a little silly) as our tribe prepared to venture into the cove.

As we were walking down to the beach, I saw a beach patrol woman and her coworker overlooking the beach.

She was intensely looking through her binoculars, and as we passed I heard her say, "...Yeah, we had one die out there last week..."

I won't lie, that got my heart pumping, but I just brushed it off and thought it must be someone who was out in the ocean and didn't know how to swim. We arrived at the beach and were confidently walking to the tide pool, green face paint glowing. And suddenly, we were stopped by a lifeguard sitting on his high, wooden throne.

"Whoa, whoa, whoa. Where do you guys think you're going?" he asked.

"We're just going down over to the tide pool to check it out and jump in," Jake responded.

The lifeguard exploded at his remark. "You think you can just walk over here with your warrior face paint acting all big and bad? This isn't a game! A boy died in there last week! Do you understand? Technically, I can't stop you guys from going over there, but I'm going to have to call you in and put patrol on alert."

I forgot what was said after that, but he definitely did his duty of striking fear into us. I was a little shaken, my mind blank with surprise. But somehow that didn't deter Jake from leading us into battle. He was smug with confidence and was determined to show us that the cove lived up to the epic hype.

When we arrived at the cove, we looked down at the swirling waters. Jake gave us a quick rundown of how to stay safe in the water. Basically, the water would come rushing in causing a swell, and that's how you jumped in and got out. It would push you back a little, so you would have to do a little bit of paddling to move forward. When the water drained out, it would push you forward and the water level would drop, so you would have to wait for the next swell. Oh, and you had to avoid getting thrown against the rocks so you wouldn't become unconscious. Jake told us that a key point was to stay calm and tread while the water was low and focus on swimming in the swell.

Naturally, we wanted to see how it was done before we tried it, and Jake jumped right in followed by a couple of my other friends. I watched them do it, and they all got in and out with ease. Next was Garrett's turn. He decided to take the cliff-jumping route, and he plunged into the water with such pizzazz. Of course if Garrett did the cliff jump, I had to do it as well. There was no way I was missing out on a thrill like that. I climbed up on the narrow ledge and stared at the water below. I took a deep breath, mustered up my courage, and tossed my body in.

I burst to the surface of the water feeling the adrenaline pour over me. I looked around with a big smile on my face and observed the faces of my friends. I let the tide pull me in and push me out a couple times and carefully tread around the rock Jake told us to look out for. Only a few seconds after I began to enjoy the swim were my worst fears realized. For some reason, the time that I decided to jump in was also the time that a huge tide decided to make an appearance. How convenient.

When I saw the huge swell approaching, I didn't need convincing to know that it was time to get out. Remembering Jake's instructions, I started making my way over to the side where I could get out. But the tide had other plans. Unfortunately for me, the swell had just reached me, and I was violently pushed in and out. I began to swim hard, attempting to grab onto the rock and pull myself out. I tried three or four times to grab on to the rock, each time waiting for the water to push me up. Each attempt was a failure. My strength was weakening as I gave my best effort to get out, but nothing was working.

Panic started to set in as I knew that my efforts were getting me nowhere. My heart started to pound in fear, which caused my body to become more fatigued. I started to slow down, drifting farther from the edge. My body was being harshly moved by the tide, and I began to worry about the rock behind me. Oh no, the lifeguard was right. I walked here thinking I was a warrior, but I'm actually a helpless teenager at the mercy of the ocean. That's when the fear of death kicked in. I came to the realization that I could actually die in this cove. I could drown or get my head thrown against a rock and sink to the bottom.

To lighten the mood even further, I decided to look up at my friends, half out of fear and half out of subconsciously giving them a final, fleeting "goodbye" glance. I have never seen faces more terrified and petrified than in that moment. No scary movie could even come close to bringing out the horrified looks they had on their faces. That pretty much sealed my death sentence in my mind. It frightened me knowing that the situation was just as chaotic and threatening as it seemed. I was nearing the point of giving up, but I managed to muster up the energy for one final, big push to free myself.

This time, I gathered all the energy I had left and swam with all my might, throwing myself onto the ledge. I still would have missed the mark if it wouldn't have been for Jake. I was going for the ledge, but instead he swooped in and grabbed my hand, pulling me up to a position where I could hoist myself up. I collapsed on the edge, gasping for air. I had made it; I would live to see another day. To be honest, I probably would not have made it if Jake hadn't made the decision that he was going to also risk slipping in by helping me up. Everyone's faces were still concerned, but the fear I saw in their eyes had gone. I was finally on land, I was safe from the currents, and I would live to tell the harrowing story.

That was the closest point to death I have ever been. I've never panicked more than I have in that moment, but shockingly, it was an experience I was glad I took part in. Jake was fearless in leading us to that spot, because he knew in the end that we would all come out okay. He had done this before and would at least be able to calm us if we encountered trouble. Jake knew that there were major risks associated with jumping into the water, but he also knew that the reward would greatly outweigh the risks. After going through that, I couldn't agree more. A lot of people will think that's crazy to say, but surviving that situation told me that if I could endure that predicament, then I could endure anything life throws at me.

A common phrase I'm sure you've heard in your life is "If your friends jumped off a bridge, would you jump off too?" And in this case, I did. Except it was a cliff that had raging currents below. (Disclaimer: I do not encourage this activity, and you should always make safe decisions, including listening to angry lifeguards.) Jake led us to this place for a reason, and if he jumped in that water, then I was going to jump in right after him.

Jake risked his life to pull me out of the water. He could've lost his footing and slipped in, or my weight could have pulled him in along with me. He saw me desperately struggling and offered a way out. Without Jake's hand grabbing me, I know I would not have been able to make it out by myself. I was helpless without someone there to rescue me.

Following Jesus is a risk. It can cause you to be uncomfortable in certain situations, you might look foolish in the eyes of others, you lose your life for the sake of him, and others might oppress you. Even considering these risks along with others, the reward of following him greatly outweighs the risks. Jesus promises us that when we lose our lives for him, we will find what life was created to be. He promises us an eternal life and eternal friendship when we grab his hand and head into the raging currents with him.

There was a time when Jesus invited his friend Peter to walk out on the water with him. Jesus's friends were terrified that he was walking on the water; they thought he was a ghost. When Jesus showed Peter that he was walking fine and asked Peter to come, Peter began to walk on the water. It was a windy day – the winds were probably as pushy as the currents I was in. Once Peter felt these winds, he became afraid and started to sink. Jesus had to reach out and grab him. Maybe that was my problem. When I saw how strong the currents were, I became fearful and lost my faith that I could do it. I needed someone else to help pull me out.

Life is full of a lot of currents and winds that will push you around and cause you to be disheartened, but Jesus isn't afraid. He leads by example and shows us that if we just have faith, we'll be able to endure the storms. When we do get caught up in the currents, he is our rescuer. He is quick to catch us and reach out his hand to pull us through tough situations. With Jesus, we aren't helpless. He doesn't leave us to fend for ourselves when we agree to follow his example. Many times, there are situations that we simply can't make it through on our own, and Jesus is the one to be there to rescue us.

Friends do crazy things together, like cliff jumping into dangerous water, but in addition to the crazy times, our friends may have times in their lives where they are being bombarded with hardships. We look down at them from the edge and see them working tirelessly to escape the traps they're held in. All they need is someone to reach down and help give them a pull out. You might take some risks by reaching out your hand, and it might take all your strength to get them to safety. Yet, the reward of the love that stems from that support will make it seem like the risk wasn't even a risk at all.

Friends are rescuers, and they risk their lives for the benefit of their own friends. Jesus says that there is no greater love than laying down your life for your friends. Rescuing your friends won't always involve a life or death situation, but laying down your life means providing every form of emotional and physical help you can give them. Pour into your friends when they don't have faith that they can make it out of the current, and they may become sharp enough to know they can make it out if they get caught in another current. Your friendship will become stronger, your friends will find faith in themselves, and the waters will become a little easier to swim in.

Chapter 4
NICE CALVES

Running is one of my least favorite things to do. First, I have asthma, so that already complicates the situation. Second, I don't have the endurance. I'm sure if I worked at it long enough, I could build my endurance. But I'm never determined enough to run long distance. I'm great at short sprints because I have the speed and a fierce competitive spirit to drive me to win; but never the desire to run anything past that.

My buddy Logan loves to run, and he's stellar at it. He constantly places within the top rankings in all the races he participates in. Although running isn't my forte, I do love to camp. During the hot summer months, Logan decided that he wanted to run a 30K at Colorado Bend State Park in Bend, Texas. The marathon was a trail run, which meant the terrain would make the race more challenging. After completing the race in the evening, the runners were allowed to camp out in one of the available spots. My friend Alec and I were invited along to watch him race.

Alec and I were eager to watch Logan compete, so we spent a day of preparation ahead of the race, preparing signs for Logan. We printed a map online and planned out a few spots we could walk to where Logan would see us while he was running. At those spots, we could cheer him on and also provide him more water and Gatorade. Alec and I came up with a few different signs that had clever puns on them, but my favorite was a sign that had baby cows on it and read "Nice Calves". Just for the record, Logan does indeed have nice calves.

The day of the race, the temperature was nearing a hundred degrees, which could present some serious problems for a runner. The race began near sunset, so the temperature would go down slightly, but not by much. Before the race, we set up camp and prepared our food so that when the race was over, we would be ready to eat and enjoy the rest of the night. We headed to the starting line, and I wondered how Logan would be able to finish. If I attempted something like this, it would take me all night to cross the finish line.

After a half hour of anticipation, the race finally began. Alec and I quickly discussed going to our first checkpoint where we would meet Logan. Amusingly, we ran there because we were afraid he might beat us there. We had the Gatorade and water ready to hand off when he passed, and the first time, we waited a while before he ran by. Finally, Alec and I heard voices in the trees, and we pulled out a megaphone we brought, ready to shout encouragement to him. We got a few chuckles out of him from our "Nice Calves" sign, and we held out his water for him to grab on his way. At the first checkpoint, he was about in 20th place.

There were four other checkpoints we planned on the path, and Logan was speeding by each one. At every meeting place, we had to run beside him in order to give him his water so we didn't slow him down. As we awaited him at the spots, we noticed he was progressively gaining ground on the other racers. He went from 20th place to 10th place to 7th to 3rd, and at our last spot before the finish line, he was neck and neck with another runner. All the other runners had become fatigued, but Logan pressed on. By this time it was dark, and we anxiously awaited him at the finish line. Logan had a chance to win the entire race, and we wondered whether he would be able to keep pace with the guy running next to him.

Time passed, and it was taking way too long for them to cross the finish line. Alec and I wondered if something had happened to them or if they took the wrong trail. Anxiously awaiting him, we finally saw a glimmer of hope in the distance. That glimmer of hope was the faint light of someone's headlamp. Like a firefly, it was weaving in and out of the trees, disappearing for a moment and reappearing with a quick flash. As the light exited the trees and made its way onto the main path, we noticed that it was the only light. This person was the clear winner – either it was Logan or his fellow runner.

The light grew closer, and we still couldn't tell who it was. Nevertheless, cheers erupted for the person who would soon be the winner. A few more strides of the runner's legs

hit the dirt, and we could just make out the figure of the
runner. By his height and the anatomy of his calves, the
runner was unquestionably none other than Logan! Alec and
I burst into a frenzy of joyful screams as Logan trotted across
the finish line. He had just won his first place finish in a half
marathon!

Logan was greeted with congratulations and awarded a
medal along with a first place decoration. He had outrun the
guy he was neck and neck with by a full minute. Logan was
once in 20th place at the first checkpoint, but had finished
over a whole hour ahead of the person who actually finished
in 20th place. We went over to his truck, and he collapsed in
the bed and caught his breath before he was ready to return to
camp. We cooked our dinner, and he passed out in the tent
before I even finished eating.

During that race, Logan never gave up, and nothing
slowed him down. He started off a little bit behind, but he
didn't let that discourage him from pressing on. Through the
two hours, forty-one minutes, and twenty-five seconds it took
him to finish, Logan was persistent. I'm sure that he was just
as fatigued as the other runners, but he kept his legs moving.
Logan wasn't focusing on how bad his legs hurt, the sweat
pouring from his body, or the rocky trail working against him
– he was focused on the finish line. He knew that by being
steady in his run, he would receive something in return; his
labor would not be in vain.

This is a wonderful example of how Jesus is persistent with us. There are times in our lives when we question him, wondering how he could allow bad things to happen to us or our friends. As a result of our questions, we lose our motivation to continuously pursue him. Even though we are fickle in our pursuit of him, Jesus never stops pursuing us. He is persistent in being present with us throughout every moment of every day. To Jesus, we are his first place prize. He wants to win our hearts over so that our spirits are fulfilled. Jesus is constant, and even when he wins our hearts over, he'll run way past the finish line. The race he runs doesn't end when we turn to him. In fact, the race will never end for him. He will persistently love us day in and day out.

The 30K that Logan ran in wasn't your average half marathon. It took place on a trail, which meant that it would be more exhausting for him to reach the finish line. The heat, rocky terrain, and elevation changes were hindrances to his completion of the race. In our friendships, there may be some hindrances that don't allow us to experience the full capacity of what it's like to love each other. The crucial point to getting through the rocky terrain is to be persistent with your friends. Friends need someone who is constant and will love them day in and day out. Even if they are angry at you, ignore you, or shut you out, the best thing you can offer them is your stable support and love. Of course, this is extremely tough to do, especially when they aren't treating you with kindness. However, when we put our selfish desires aside, we can truly fathom the love Jesus yearns for us to give.

Even though it may not seem like your persistence is paying off in your friendship, Jesus tells us that it will. He tells us that when we ask, it will be given to us. When we knock on the door, it will open. Spend some time searching, and you'll find it. Ask Jesus for a way to soften your friends' hearts, search for a way to love them the way they need to be loved, and knock on their door to tell them you're still there. It can be tiring, but when you finally cross that finish line, beating all the odds by an incredible time, you'll be the sharpest set of tools in the box.

Chapter 5

FRAXES

I think the hottest summer I've experienced was during my junior year of high school during the summer months of band camp. I'm a music nerd, and I played the mellophone in the marching band. For those of you who don't know what a mellophone is, it's the marching version of the French horn. Imagine it as an enlarged version of a trumpet. At the end of July, we would go to band camp where we would practice long hours in the summer heat to prepare for our competition a few months later.

Besides the blistering heat that drained me of life, there was something else I really enjoyed about that year. At the beginning of the year, my friend Destiny and I figured out we had the exact same schedule. Every class, every day, and every minute of school would be spent together. Destiny was also in band, so practice before and after school would add even more time to the mix, so it seemed like the only time we would be separated was when we each went home to sleep.

Destiny and I played the coolest instruments that were offered (or so our humble opinions suggested). I played the French horn, and she played the saxophone. We were both section leaders of our instrument groups, which meant we were in charge of making sure the people in our section knew their music, marching routines, and were taken care of in every way they needed. We were so excited to have new members of our section, and we wanted to make sure our sections were the best the band had.

Thinking about working individually with our sections, we hated the idea because we wanted to be together. Granted, our instruments played a lot of the same musical parts, but we also wanted to be in the same section. Before classes and band camp started, the excitement of band directed most of our conversations. Naturally, one of those conversations was about wanting to be in the same section. We were going to do everything else together, so if we could only be in the same section, everything would be perfect! Then, the solution to all of our problems came to our heads as quick as a sixteenth note. What if – now hear us out – what if we combined our sections? What if we made it so that two sections turned into one? We were two completely different instruments, one brass and the other woodwind, but that didn't matter because we played almost the same musical part. We would call our new section the "Fraxes"! A perfect combination of the French horn and sax.

We knew our band director would never approve of an official merging of the sections. What sane director would? Thus, we approved it ourselves. We made it public to the band through our obnoxious Frax chants that we had merged, but without an official stamp of approval. Even if we did get a stamp of approval, we probably still would have called ourselves the Fraxes. The first time we made our declaration that we were now one unit was at a theme day at band camp. For select days during camp, we would have a particular theme we could dress up for. The day that we "officially" dubbed ourselves the Fraxes was tribal day, and Destiny and I had prepared for this well in advance. We had ordered tribal tank tops that had our new section name and receive help in making feather headbands. That day, we became a tribe.

Being a tribe helped us out in a lot of ways that year. In order to be successful as a band, the band needs to be cohesive musically and relationally. By building strong and meaningful relationships, the band has more motivation and subconscious chemistry to work together while marching. Becoming our tribe helped unify the band even further, and we were able to put in a lot of good work. It wasn't all dandelions and sunshine, but we did form an atypical bond. Our tribe not only worked well with each other, but with the other sections as well. As a result, we all put in such great work that we were able to advance to the state competition – something the high school band hadn't seen in many years.

The remarkable memories with Destiny that year were innumerable. Spending a lot of time with someone, as you can imagine, yields many unforgettable moments. Our creation of the Fraxes wasn't just something we made so we could spend more time together. It was a symbol of our unbreakable bond. It was a commitment to be loyal against all odds and a statement of our inseparability. We were a tribe committed to be reliable, dependable, and trustworthy.

Destiny and I are two completely different characters, but somehow we made a great team. During that year, she entrusted her loyalty to me, and it payed off tremendously. We excelled in our extracurricular activities, developed a deep friendship, and I acquired a companion that I could go to for anything. I knew that whatever was thrown my way, she would be there behind me to have my back.

Jesus is the most loyal companion we could ever have. He wants to be with you every minute of every day, but we fall very short of constantly acknowledging him every day. Sometimes our lives become so busy and filled with activity that Jesus completely slips our mind. Regardless of our failures, he is present with us wherever we go. Jesus wants to be so close to you that your bond is unbreakable. He wants there to be no you without him and no him without you. Through your commitment to him, he wants others to see him in you.

As humans, we are destined to fail. There are times when we become unfaithful to our friends and even to Jesus, but Jesus will never be unfaithful. Even when we think we've finally done it – we've done "that thing" that will surely cause Jesus to reject us, he is always true to us and loves us unconditionally. We may be so angry or ashamed that we don't want his love, but it is there for us nonetheless. There is nothing we could ever do that can separate us from his love.

Loyalty without action is meaningless. You can say you're loyal to your friend time and time again, but they will never believe you unless you show them. You show your friends loyalty through commitment, selflessness, and protection. You commit your time, resources, and energy to them. You set aside your own desires so that they can benefit instead. You protect them from harm and affliction that tries to topple them over.

Jesus tells us that in order for us to be loyal to him, we need to deny ourselves and pick up our cross. Rather than asking for a verbal commitment, he is asking us for action. He requests us to put down our selfishness, pride, and greediness so we can experience his grace. The crazy thing is, even if we are arrogant enough to not put down these things, he will still offer us his grace. We are undeserving, yet he still generously gives it with open hands. Friendships aren't one way; it brings Jesus overwhelming joy when we simply do what he asks by denying ourselves. We aren't asked to take the easy way out, but we are asked to be willing to die for his sake. We are asked to fully surrender to his instruction for our lives. Of course, that's a tremendous thing to ask of someone. But isn't that what loyalty is?

To be loyal to a friend, you don't have to spend time with them twenty-four hours a day, seven days a week. That's not the kind of commitment loyalty entails. Although that would be a killer friendship if you were able to do that, you might be driven insane if you had to spend every waking minute with your friend. Loyalty is looking out for your friend's best interests and giving constant support.

Without loyalty, we become drifters. Drifters are people who come in and out of your life in random spurts. They stay when it's easy, but when there's a challenge presented, they leave as quickly as they came. Having drifter friends doesn't feel good, and it isn't pleasant to others either. As painless as it is to be a drifter, being loyal empowers your friends to live life, reaching beyond what they ever dreamed of being capable of, because they know they have a safety net to fall on – you.

Chapter 6
I TOLD YOU SNOW

If you've ever had the privilege to ski, you know it's no easy task the first time. Your legs shake more than a maraca during an earthquake. Steering yourself in the right direction is also a sight to behold. Unfortunately, you can't simply look right and expect to go right. Shifting your weight between your legs is a factor in how your body will turn. Of course, this could all just be me. Maybe it's actually not as hard as I'm describing. All I know is that when I wanted to turn right, I would go left, and there were way too many face-plants to be deemed healthy.

For a spring break vacation, my friends and I decided to go to Colorado to explore the natural beauty and embark on a skiing adventure. For most people in our posse, skiing was a completely new glass of tea. But for Jack, it was almost routine. I'm pretty sure if he wanted to, he could ski backwards on one leg, balance a Jenga tower on his head, all while texting me how good he is at skiing. He has been on his fair share of ski trips, and to the rest of us, he was a legend in the folklore of the skiing kingdom.

I think if anyone saw me during my first attempt at standing up and sliding down the slope, I think they would describe it as a praying mantis attempting to karate chop a peanut in mid-air. In simpler terms, I was a disaster. Thankfully, I wasn't alone in this; most of my friends were in similar situations. I will admit they were a little bit more graceful than me; they looked more like swans than praying mantises.

Because of our clumsiness, Jack offered to help teach us how to ski. It's a good thing he did, otherwise I would be screaming like a piglet going down the slopes, fearing for my life. But the humor doesn't stop there. Jack is a trial and error sort of guy; if you get my drift. Don't get me wrong, he is very efficient in giving instructions, but when he gives them once, it's time to put it to the test. He gives no repeats or different instructions, just minor tips that could help you along the way. He'll kind of look at you with a grin, shrug, and then say, "Eh, just go for it!" For some reason, hearing that from Jack is enough advice, and you end up going for it. As you can imagine, that made for some spectacular crashes.

When you're on the slopes, they label the different paths in terms of difficulty. Green are the easiest, followed by blue for intermediates, and black for the most difficult. When I got on my first green, adrenaline was pulsing through my veins. I wanted to go as fast as I could down the slope and look like I'd been doing it for years. I drove my ski poles into the ground and catapulted myself forward with a single push. It was all going perfectly; I was beginning to gain speed, and I hadn't even lost my balance. I knew that this was my time to show the world I was an Olympian. I was born for this. As if hearing my unbreakable ego, the mountain decided to push me down. I could've made it to the bottom unscathed if the mountain didn't keep tripping me. Unfortunately, my entire descent looked like that. I would be a cool skier for a few seconds, fall on my face, be a cool skier for a few seconds, and fall on my back. Rinse and repeat.

After a couple hours of tolerating the novices, the flavorless simplicity of it all became too much for an accomplished connoisseur such as Jack, and he needed something with a little more zest. What better way to appease a crackerjack than to provide him with a smorgasbord of challenging and invigorating inclines? This is what the locals would call the blue slopes. By this point, I had become comfortable with skiing down the greens and rarely took falls. It was only my first time skiing, so I didn't want to rush anything if I wasn't ready for it. Then again, heroes weren't born for mediocrity. I decided to join him on the blues and take the next step in becoming a historic Olympian.

We took the lift up to the top of one of the blue slopes, and I got a little jittery. It was a big difference from where we had been before: higher, steeper, and more twists than the greens. What was there to be afraid of? After a few hours of skiing, I labeled myself as an intermediate – I could handle the pressure. Arriving at the top, I dismounted the lift and lost my balance, causing me to topple over. I told myself not to worry. I had to get it out of my system while I still could, because this slope was for the veteran elite. I had mastered the greens in a single day, so naturally, I belonged in the elite club.

Standing at the crest of the hill, I stood by Jack looking down at the smooth snow encasing the incline. To my surprise, Jack began instructing me, and when he starts giving you pointers after he's already taught you some things, you better listen up because it's probably important.

"So on these, you want to snake your way down. You want to make wide turns to avoid gaining too much speed," he said.

Great, I could do that in my sleep. Wide turns and slow down. Got it! As fast as a viper strikes its prey, Jack began snaking his way down.

"Alright, here we go," I thought to myself.

With a deep breath, I slid on the path, ready to show the blue what I was made of. The rush of excitement was nearly overwhelming. Even while winding my way down, I could gain speed quickly. I had to put my skis horizontal to the slope a few times in order to slow myself to a comfortable speed. Wow, I had made it. I was a pro. But then I saw Jack doing his thing. He was weaving in between people like a gopher sprinting through its tunnels. I was losing ground on him, too. I had to catch up, and I had to show him that I could be a speedster.

It was time to unleash my full potential and unlock the true power within. I was going to beat him to the bottom, and there would be no one who could stop me. I increased my speed dramatically in an effort to overtake my master. I could hear and feel the wind whistling past my ears, and I turned my skis straight downward. I was alive and thriving, watching the people around me whiz out of my view. With every second, Jack was getting closer and closer. Finally, he was within my range. I kept going full speed ahead like a wasp pinpointing its target to sting. With a determined and smug grin, I overtook Jack and claimed my winning title. My competitive spirit was completely satisfied, and I swooshed left and right like a bona fide professional.

They say pride comes before the fall, and I was a living example. Without warning, my title was stripped from me, and I tumbled down like a ragdoll. I would ask you to pity me, but it was such a hilarious sight, I would not be offended if anyone laughed. After a few rolls, I began to panic because the rolling didn't stop. I tried to claw at the snow, but my efforts were in vain. At last, I got my skis to dig into the snow, grinding me into a halt. I sat there breathless, laughing at my naïve determination.

A guy that was stopped a few feet away looked at me with a slight amusement glimmering in his eyes and asked, "You good, man?"

Before I could respond, the look in his eyes changed from delight to concern. He was looking behind me, as if something was swiftly approaching. "Oh no, Oh no, Oh no…" he mumbled.

Instantly, I knew what was happening. I heard the sound of skis gliding across the snow right behind me. I knew that someone was going to run straight into me, and frankly, I deserved it. I grimaced and prepared for impact. Just as I saw the shadow of the skier behind me, I felt a shower of cold snow shroud my body and land on my head. There was no collision, and the skier zoomed around me like I was nothing. He looked back and gave me wide grin, as if to say, "I told you snow". Yes, I used that dad pun because the person who gave me the snow shower I rightfully deserved was none other than the king of dad jokes himself: Jack. I looked at the guy next to me, shaking my head with a smile, and he laughed at my predicament. I continued down the rest of the mountain cautiously, accepting my humble place on the blue slope.

Sacrificing some of his personal ski time for the sake of me and my friends, Jack took on the role of a teacher. He could have easily left us, gone his own way, and enjoyed his ski time doing more challenging courses. Instead, he decided it was important to ensure that the rest of us reached a point where we also enjoyed the experience. He guided us into doing the right things by watching over us and giving us advice when we fell. Jack even had a sense of humor when I strayed from his teachings. He didn't become angry or annoyed that I was doing it wrong, but he knew it was a mistake made from a naïve heart.

Jesus was the ultimate example of a teacher. He traveled around with his disciples telling parables and being an example of how to live a good life. Jesus taught the people he encountered with passion. In Mark 6, it says that Jesus saw the crowds and they looked like sheep without a shepherd. That's exactly what we probably looked like to Jack. Lost, confused, and clumsy skiers without direction or someone to herd them. Jesus felt for these lost people and became the person they most needed – a shepherd to watch over them and gently lead them in the right direction.

If Jesus wanted to, he could have easily commanded everyone to live as he told them to. He has all the power, so why didn't he just use his power to make us do what he wanted us to do? The reason is because that's not what love is, and he wouldn't be a very good teacher if he forced us into anything. An important part of teaching is to let your students learn, and learning involves trial and error. Jesus wants us to choose to follow him, and that means that as humans we will inevitably make mistakes. Yet, Jesus loves us and continues to guide us through those mistakes. We will fall over and over again, but Jesus is right there to pick us up and give us pointers for the next attempt.

Of course, some of those falls will be accidents, but others will also be on purpose. We'll deliberately disobey or ignore his teachings and decide to ski down the slope as fast and as wildly as we can for the fun of it. But Jesus knows a lot better than we do, and sometimes he even has a sense of humor about it. He knows that we'll try some funny business and occasionally, gently let you know that he told you so. Jesus never becomes annoyed that we're "doing it wrong". All he wants is for us to make an effort to follow him and listen to his guidance.

Sometimes, your friends may be going through a situation where they look like a lost sheep. They're in need of guidance and for someone to instruct them how to not slip down and fall. Maybe it's not even that deep. Maybe your friends are struggling in learning a new skill. Whatever the circumstances, good friends are good teachers. To sharpen your friends, you need to be able to see the potential in them and bring that potential out of them by giving them the knowledge you possess. If you've been down a similar path that they're experiencing, you should be quick to guide them. Be a teacher to your friends so that you can learn from each other and be apt for challenges in a world filled with slippery slopes.

Chapter 7

PACK A SWEATER

Everyone has that one place that they've always wanted to visit, but they may not ever get around to doing it because of time, money, or other obstacles. I've been to Colorado, but I've always wanted to go to Denver. Everything about it sounds magical to me: the city in the mountains, the mile-high elevation, my favorite football team, unique food, the airport, and the Red Rocks Amphitheater nearby. I could go on forever about what there is to love about Denver. Unfortunately, I hadn't been able to go because I was a college student with a tight budget on a tight schedule.

Being a student and working is tough, and sometimes the employment work on top of the school work can really weigh down on you. I was having one of those days where the weight was really pressing down hard. I worked a long shift at the finance department at the business school, and I had an extreme headache. I was in a bad mood, tired, and didn't want to talk to anyone. Furthermore, it was hot outside and the twenty-five minute walk home didn't do my mood any favors. Thankfully, when I arrived at our apartment, there was no one home. I could plop down in bed, take a nap, and let my mind rest.

I made my way up the creaky stairs to my loft room and flipped on the light. Something was different than I left it. Someone had definitely been in my room. On my bed was one of my orange Denver Broncos shirts. I didn't remember leaving it there; in fact, I was almost positive that I folded it and put it away. I walked over to the shirt, put my backpack down, and discovered a note on top of the shirt. "Put this on," it read. That was a strange request, but I figured I would play along. I was almost positive that one of my roommates was going to jump out in a football jersey of their own and tackle me. So I put the shirt on, and noticed at the bottom of the note, it said, "Go to 2 Corinthians 1:3-4". I opened my Bible, which was conveniently placed on the bed, and turned to the verse that was boxed out in pen. The verses said, "Praise be to the God and Father of our Lord Jesus Christ, the Father of compassion and the God of all comfort, who comforts us in all our troubles, so that we can comfort those in any trouble with the comfort we ourselves receive from God." Next to the verse was written: "Last page of your journal". Okay, I admit this was fun, and I was ready to see what was at the end of this.

I opened to the back of my journal, and on the last page was written, "Pack a sweater and your beanie. YOU ARE GOING TO a Broncos Game w/ me! -Cody". Placed neatly in the page were two tickets to a Broncos game. My friend and roommate Cody had just bought us tickets to an actual game in Denver. It was actually happening! I was going to go to Denver. So many things were going through my head at that point. I felt silly for being in a bad mood and having my demeanor completely flip around. How could Cody be so generous as to buy that for me? Where was he? I was going to tackle him in a hug and scold him at the same time! He should not have done that; he could have used the money for something more important. With an excited grin, I grabbed my phone to text him to get home as soon as possible.

When Cody arrived home, I tackled him in a big hug and shouted thank you more times in a minute than is humanly possible. I asked him why he did that, and he said because he knew I really wanted to go and that it would be fun. I was astounded that he would choose to do that just because it was something I wanted to do. After that, we planned our trip and I was ready to go. However, I couldn't go just yet. It was only September, and the game was on New Year's Eve, so we wouldn't even be in Denver until December 30th.

December 30th finally rolled around, and it was time to board our flight to Denver. I was probably annoying Cody with how giddy I was, but I didn't care. I was about to head to the city I had always dreamed of visiting. When we arrived in Denver, it exceeded all of my expectations. It almost seemed like I was made to be there. I'm more of a nature-lover than a city-lover, but the buildings and surroundings of Denver are stunning! The second day, I got to attend the Broncos game sitting at the top of the stadium. It was a great game even though the Broncos lost, and the snow during the game made up for the loss (even though I could see Cody internally screaming to leave). That night, we got to go see the fireworks show in the heart of Denver for the New Year's celebration. If you've never seen fireworks in a city before, I highly recommend putting that on your to-do list – it's quite a sight!

Denver delivered all that I thought it would and more. The experiences in the thin, cold air is something I will never forget, and all of this was made possible because Cody gave it to me. The money he used for us to have an electrifying experience in a city I wanted to explore could have been used for so many different things. He could have spent it on something he wanted to do, but instead he decided to check something off for me on my bucket list. Cody is a generous dude, and he makes sure that people are cared for by surprising them with little things. Except this time, this was no little thing. His generosity exploded just like the fireworks we watched in downtown Denver. Not only is Cody generous in the material things he gives, he is also generous with his love for others.

When Jesus was teaching how to give, he told the people to give humbly and without a fanfare showing people what you give. I like to think of this as gentle giving. There is something about gentle people that captivates the hearts of others. A soft spirit combined with a natural generosity is something that's rarely seen. This is the way Jesus gave, and it's the way he wants us to give as well. He didn't perform miracles to show off or prove his capability to others, but he did it because he wanted to see people blossom and live their wildest dreams. The blind wanted to see, so he gave them sight; the sick wanted to be healed, so he cured them; and the hungry wanted to be fed, so he provided. They were ordinary people with dreams of the unimaginable, and Jesus, with his gentle spirit, made these dreams come true through his generosity.

Proverbs 11:24-25 states, "One gives freely, yet gains even more; another withholds unduly, but comes to poverty. A generous person will prosper; whoever refreshes others will be refreshed." Not only does Jesus want us to give with a gentle spirit, but he wants us to give freely and without bound. Taken literally, the first verse is confusing. How can you give away your possessions and gain more? If you hold everything for yourself, how can you lose it and be reduced to poverty? This isn't talking about material possessions, it's talking about our hearts. When you give things away, it will make you feel good because you'll see that it makes the other person feel good. If your heart is selfish, you'll become cold, and your heart will be drained. Giving requires that we release all of our desires, pride, and impulses to open our closed hands.

When we are generous, we don't live in the fashion we previously lived. Because of the outpouring of our hearts, we will prosper, flourish, and be overwhelmed by receiving a sense of love. By refreshing others, we will be refreshed. I love the idea of giving being compared to refreshing because that's what it feels like to give. To refresh means to give new strength or energy to, or to reinvigorate. We get a new excitement and energy from seeing the light in people's eyes when they receive an outpouring of love, kind of like going to the beach and taking a deep breath of the salty sea air. We don't get enough of it, but we absolutely need more of it.

Jesus is generous in what he gives to us. Just take a minute to sit and think of all the things you've been blessed with; you probably can list off a lot more things than you initially thought. One thing that Jesus always gives generously without end is his love for us. He is described as living water, pouring and flowing with an endless supply of refreshing love. You don't even have to ask for it because he's constantly giving it to you. Think of it in this way: You have a friend who follows you around everywhere, and every second that passes he gives you a dollar. That would be absolutely insane! You would be given $86,400 per day! You'd be rich! Chances are you don't have a friend who gives you a dollar a day, but Jesus is constantly giving us love every second of every day. He allows us to be rich in his love, and it's better than money could ever be.

Being a friend means that you are a gentle giver, allowing your hands and spirit to be generous and free. Although a small material gift every once in a while doesn't hurt, the point is not to give in this regard. The point is to have love flowing from you like a mighty waterfall. Invite your friends into your life, home, and journey with Jesus. Enriching your friends' lives in this way will not only foster joy within them but will permit you to experience a newfound joy yourself. Attaching yourself to material possessions and always focusing attention on yourself can ultimately lead you to become bitter and closed off to others. Generosity is not only a tool for sharpening, but for shining. The outpour that your friends receive from a gracious heart will cause them to light up and become an ironwork that is keen and glowing with fulfillment.

Chapter 8

BLOOD, SWEAT, AND TEARS

My ears popped, and I became sleepy as we reached our peak altitude on our flight home. I was on my way home with my church friends coming back from a trip to Peru. It had been a long, laborious trip, and we were all ready to get some rest. I was sitting by my friends Jake and Reagan, and although we were tired, we weren't quite ready for sleep. We looked around the plane, and all of our friends were passed out. We twiddled our thumbs in boredom, and we finally decided to play games.

Just as a precursor, I generally do great with altitude. I'm able to breathe fine, I don't get lightheaded, and I never get nosebleeds. However, for some reason, this time the altitude wanted to show me who was boss. Jake, Reagan, and I were minding our own business playing our game and laughing. After a while of playing the game, I caught the sniffles. I thought to myself that it must be allergies. There were probably a few allergens from Peru that my body wasn't used to, so I didn't think too much into it. However, the drainage in my nose kept wanting to come out, so I had to keep sniffling. It wasn't until I stopped sniffling that I realized what it was.

Oozing from my nostrils was exactly what I'd never thought it would be: blood. At first I wasn't too concerned. Reagan and Jake suggested that I lean my head back and squeeze my nose for a few minutes, so I took their advice and tried this method. After a few minutes, I released my nose and tilted my head back down. It had worked! Well, at least for five seconds. Just as I was about to be comforted by the absence of red fluid leaving my body, here it came again. This time, it was even worse than before. It wasn't just a stream; it was like Niagara Falls had decided to release all its splendor in the form of blood through my nose.

It was an uncontrollable nightmare as blood flowed down my chin and onto my shirt. As much as I tried to stop it, it just kept streaming. I don't know why, but in crisis situations I like to laugh. I don't know if laughing is my body's natural response to ease the stress of the situation, but it works. While the chaos was ensuing, I looked over at Jake in desperation hoping that he had something to help me stop the blood. However, I guess my maniacal appearance triggered him to laugh, and he doubled over in a laughing fit. I turned to Reagan, and she struck a similar pose. She had her mouth wide open, and she was laughing so hard that no sound was coming out. By the looks of it, this wasn't going to get better anytime soon.

I began to sweat out of nervousness for the debacle to stop, and I decided to take matters into my own hands. With vigor, I frantically pressed the call button for the flight attendant, hoping for some form of help. Then, the worst thing that could possibly happen happened. I felt a slight tickling sensation in the upper chambers of the old breather, and there was no containing its vicious wrath. With a single explosion, I sneezed a ghastly amount of blood onto the back of the seat in front of me. The area was that of a crime scene: blood on my face, on my hands, and splattered on the seat in front of me. It looked like I had just committed a very graphic crime. After a couple minutes, a flight attendant approached our row. Initially, he looked at Jake, but Jake was laughing too hard to even clearly explain the situation to him. Following a look of confusion, he looked down the row for clarification. I'll never forget the look of sheer terror that slipped across his face as he looked at me and then bolted down the aisle. That look almost made me think I was a dangerous criminal.

I must've looked really pitiful during those ten minutes of catastrophe. There was blood spewing from my face, I was layered in a thin coat of sweat, and tears were streaming from my eyes from laughter. In my disarray, what were Jake and Reagan doing? Laughing. Although, with my pathetic (and admittedly humorous) appearance, I really don't blame them. I was at least glad to have friends who were making light of the situation. Finally, the concerned flight attendant rushed back with a stack of napkins, and I clogged my nose full of them. The bleeding stopped shortly after, and all was right in the world.

Jake and Reagan weren't too concerned in this situation. Instead, they had humor and made light of it. They knew that it wasn't that serious and that everything was going to turn out okay in the end. They trusted that there was someone on the plane that would be able to help me. So instead of being afraid or frustrated that there was someone profusely bleeding next to them, they turned their hearts to laughter. They laughed at my inability to control myself and the mess I was clumsily trying to get out of.

Believe it or not, Jesus had a couple moments like this. Don't get me wrong, Jesus is a helper in our time of need, and he wouldn't ever laugh at us if we were actually hurt. The story I'm thinking of is when a few of Jesus's disciples went out to fish one night after Jesus had risen from the dead. It was probably a long and frustrating night. The disciples fished all night and caught nothing. I can only imagine the chaos on the boat as they got frustrated with one another because they couldn't catch anything. I imagine them frantically throwing their nets in and pulling them out as they hoped to catch a single fish. They might've gone a little whacko and yelled, saying, "Come on! Just one fish is all I want!"

The disciples put their blood, sweat, and tears into catching fish, yet they didn't catch a single one. Then, as the sun begins to rise, Jesus decides to go check on his disciples to see how they're doing. He walks up to the shore, probably shaking his head and smirking. He looks at them for a little bit and then shouts at them, "Hey friends! Anyone catch anything?" At this point, the disciples didn't know it was Jesus standing on the shore. They just thought it was a random stranger, and they were probably a little irritated at this guy asking them if they caught anything when clearly they didn't. They replied with a simple, "No." That reply just screams, "Get away from us! We're mad, tired, and just want to catch fish, so please leave us alone." Jesus probably chuckled to himself, and then he says, "Yeah, maybe try the other side of the boat. There's definitely fish there." If I had just gone through a night like that, and someone said that to me, my eyes would have rolled to the back of my head.

But what did they have to lose at this point? They decided to appease the man on the shore, and they likely had a little sass in their throw. When they tried to bring the net in, they couldn't even pull it into the boat because there were so many fish. Jesus's smile was wide at this point, knowing that everything would be fine when it was all said and done. His disciples finally recognized it was him and swam as fast as they could towards shore. And Jesus says, "Yeah, yeah, just bring some of those fish over here. Let's eat breakfast."

The disciples had a night full of frustration and disorder. No matter how hard they tried, their efforts produced nothing. They were probably a little worried about what they were going to eat since they didn't catch anything, and they might've been scared that their pride would be hurt because of their entire night of no results. However, Jesus knew that everything was going to be okay. He saw the situation and made light of it because he knew what the end result would be. He added a little humor to the situation to show the disciples how pointless their worries were. The disciples didn't need to be frantic because they would be taken care of.

When my nose started bleeding, I was a little fearful because I thought I might get blood everywhere. It had never happened before, which caused my frantic, hectic behavior. I was also scared that I might be a little embarrassed because of the mess I had made. Although I was acting like a madman, Jake and Reagan knew I would be fine, so they made light of the situation. They knew that in the end, I would be taken care of. They looked at me knowing I was making a big deal out of something that was miniscule.

A lot of times we may find ourselves in situations that seem overwhelming, frenzied, and may leave us feeling embarrassed. We put so much emphasis on small things that don't even matter. When you step back and look at the bigger picture, putting so much weight on such insignificant issues can cause us a lot of undue stress. We pour our blood, sweat, and tears into something (literally, in my case), only to see that we'll achieve the same result if we had only remained calm and believed that we would be okay in the end. If we take a deep breath and make light of the situation, we might avoid being too dramatic.

Jesus never thinks any of our problems are too small, but he does want us to know that we'll be taken care of. When

I'm stressing over something that I shouldn't be, I know that he's saying, "Oh, Caleb. If only you knew." When I think about all the little things that I lost it over, every single time it worked out. When we trust Jesus with the big issues, we should also trust him with the smaller ones. The small problems should feel a whole lot different than the big ones. When we try to do life by our own accord, we fail a lot more times than we like to admit. Jesus knows that we're just fishing in the wrong spot. Just on the other side of the boat are the fish that Jesus gives us to say, "You're going to be okay."

What I'm not trying to say is laugh at all your friend's problems. Instead, we should be there to tell them that everything will work out for them. Oftentimes, we're like Jesus on the shore. We can see our friends struggling and panicking, but we're the ones who have a clearer understanding of the solution to their difficulties. Because of our alternative perspective, we can offer them guidance on how to navigate to a resolution. When we're able to offer this advice and assure that good will come out of our predicaments, it transforms their dark reality into a light-hearted one. They're able to see the humor in the situation and know that all the things they're worried about are irrelevant in the grand scheme of things.

Jesus will take care of us. He takes care of the rest of the Earth, and you are no exception. Be the friend that transforms heavy hearts into light ones. Bring laughter into tense moments and humor when you know your friend needs a smile. Even if you're unable to help them solve their problem, they'll remember that you were sitting beside them, laughing, cry-laughing, and bringing happiness to them when they desired it most.

Chapter 9

GREEN BEANS AND A
STRANDED BOAT

My aunt has this recipe for green beans that will change your entire mindset on green vegetables. Don't like green beans? Think again, because these green beans are wrapped in bacon and covered with a brown sugar sauce that's sure to satisfy anyone. The first time I made these legendary green beans was for a Thanksgiving meal that my friends and I were having. Even though this was my first shot at glory, they totally lived up to my aunt's standard. What can I say? Bacon makes the world a better place for everyone.

This was the first time we were having a potluck meal together, and we were all gathered at Iñaki's lake house minus a couple people we were waiting on. I ended up being one of the last people to bake my dish, so I was getting a late start, but at least mine would be fresh when we started eating. Everybody was having a good time inside, and then someone had the idea to take the boat out on the lake before we ate. Since I was still cooking, I tried to convince everyone to stay until my green beans were finished, but it was no use. Like a father watching his children leave the nest, I watched as my friends piled into the boat and sailed into the vanishing twilight. I put my green beans into the oven and waited as the half hour was ticking by. I really wished that I could be on the boat with everyone, but I had hungry mouths to feed.

Suddenly, in the midst of my silence and boredom, the phone rang – it was Iñaki. At that moment, I knew there was going to be trouble. I picked up the phone and answered. Iñaki was obviously flustered, and he informed me that the boat had died in the middle of the lake. They were left stranded with no means of escape. Great! That meant I could eat all the food left over here by myself! As much as I wanted to hog the dinner, he said he had a plan of action, and it involved me. He told me I needed to look in one of the drawers for a key. But not just any key – a key to a jet ski, and I was supposed to ride it over to them so that Iñaki could tow the boat back with the jet ski. This was excellent news – especially since I had never operated a jet ski before. What could possibly go wrong?

I hung up the phone and entered immediate panic mode. I found the key, and I thought through what I needed to do. First things first, I had to get the green beans out of the oven so they wouldn't burn the whole house down while I was out. They weren't done yet, so I would have to cook them later. I opened the drawer and grabbed the oven mitts, removing my undercooked dish from the heat. Next, I needed to quickly throw on my swimming shorts. Once I did that, I scurried back into the kitchen to grab the key. There was only one problem: I forgot where I put the key down in the midst of my panic.

Well, this was just fantastic. Looks like I would get to eat all that food by myself after all. After a few frantic minutes of searching, I buried my hands in my face and accepted my fate. I lost the key, and I had to call and tell them that they were stuck. With remorse, I picked up the phone and called Iñaki. I told him the situation, and he responded with, "Are you serious?" Yep, I was dead serious. However, he had one final game plan. If this didn't work, then nothing would. He instructed me that there was one key in the jet ski, and I should use that one to try and start the engine. I hung up the phone and swallowed hard. I walked outside onto the dock and hopped on to the jet ski.

With anxiousness flowing through my veins, my trembling hands found the key, and I inserted it and attempted to start the engine. It didn't start and dread poured over me. With desperation, I attempted one more time, and miraculously, it started! We were in business, baby! With triumph, I slowly backed out of the dock and turned around to retrieve my friends. I could see them in the distance. They were a tiny, helpless speck on the horizon. At first, I was going at an extraordinarily slow speed because my inexperience of operating a jet ski made me nervous. But the further I went, the more confident I became, and I increased my speed as the wind whipped through my hair. I felt like a hero at that moment; I was going to save all my stranded friends.

As I finally got within close range of the boat, I saw my friends standing up. With a roar of applause, they cheered me on as I slowed next to the boat. They were saying things like "you saved us" and "you're the hero". Indeed, it did feel like a cheesy movie where I was the hero, and I was feeling mighty prideful about it. I turned off the engine so Iñaki could work his magic, and I stepped onto the boat with my swelling ego. I looked around and smiled at everyone, content with the fact that I had saved them, and we would all be home to eat our potluck dinner soon. I would get to bake my green beans, and everything would fall perfectly into place.

After a few minutes waiting for Iñaki to hook up the jet ski to the boat, we heard him mumbling in disbelief. In an instant, our boisterous talking turned into curious silence. With annoyance, Iñaki told us that the jet ski wasn't starting. I sunk back with disappointment, my ego now burst. Splendid. I acted like such a big shot, and now I felt like a complete idiot. I didn't save my friends, and now I was stuck in the middle of the lake with them.

We started brainstorming things to do, and we thought of calling the patrol to come rescue us. But then, Iñaki remembered that we still had people that hadn't arrived at his house yet and that he had another jet ski. Crossing our fingers, we made a phone call to our last hope: Lindsey. She

answered, and we explained the situation to her. Glory to
God. She was only a few minutes away from the house! Iñaki
told her how to start the other jet ski, and our true rescuer
would soon be there to save us from our helplessness.

A short time passed, and we see something approaching
in the distance, which of course was the heroic Lindsey. This
time, we all stood and cheered for her and cried out in
thankfulness. She was the real hero, and she was there to
safely bring us home. Iñaki made sure to leave this jet ski on
so that we didn't repeat our first mistake, and shortly after,
we were on our way back. We finally arrived back at the
house, and we laughed and recounted the somewhat hilarious
events that occurred. Then, with me feeling stupid, we all
looked for the key that I lost that could've made things a lot
more disastrous if it hadn't been for the extra key. We all
scouted the house but couldn't find it anywhere, so we gave
up.

I felt like a let-down because of that, but it was time to
finish cooking my green beans. I put them back in the oven
and let them cook, and when the timer was done, I opened
the oven mitt drawer. There, lying right in the middle of the
oven mitts was the key. Are you kidding me? In my panic
and rush to save everyone, I must have misplaced it when I
was putting the oven mitts back after I took out my green
beans! I told everyone that I had just found the key, and relief
flowed over me. I may have lost my hero title that day, but at
least I didn't permanently lose the key!

Jesus has a plan of action for us, and sometimes we can lose our way, even if we are trying our best to follow his instructions. We think we have everything figured out and that we can steal the show. We accept opportunities given to us with pride, and we think we're the hero of the day. In an instant, we can be knocked down by something out of our control and be humbled on the spot. We think we had the perfect course of action, but it turns out we were lost the entire time.

Iñaki had a firm plan of action for the boat to get back to the house, but somehow I managed to lose the key, which probably contributed to the jet ski not starting since I had to use an entirely different key. Obviously, I didn't lose the key on purpose, but it's only human nature to mess up. If I had kept a cool head and knew that Jesus was going to work it out, things might've turned out differently. Of course, it could have also been in his plan to humble me all along!

Driving the jet ski up to my friends, I had a lot of pride. It wasn't until the jet ski wouldn't start, and Lindsey had to rescue us that I realized I was not the hero. No matter how valiant I felt, I could not save them by my own strength – it was out of my control. I was not the hero that day – Lindsey was. It was by her doing that we could get back to our meal, not mine. I didn't contribute anything to the success of that rescue. All I did was add another person we had to tow back.

Many times, we think we're the hero, and we like to lean on our own understanding. If you haven't learned by now, we're not the heroes here, Jesus is. We try to steal his show when he's been the star all along. He gets the credit for being our rescuer, not us. We don't have the strength to save ourselves or others on our own. We can try, but we're simply people that are incapable of doing what only Jesus can do. In the midst of our clumsiness, he has a plan of action. Even if we screw up that plan, he will still come zooming in on a majestic jet ski, ready to bring us home where we belong. When we let him be the hero, we're never really stranded.

In our lives, we need to let friends be the heroes. Did you get that? I said we need to let friends be the heroes, not us. Sure, you're probably capable of some really cool things, but no one wants to be around someone who is always flaunting their gifts or bragging about themselves around the clock. To be good friends, we need to shine the spotlight on them and take it off us. In fact, one day we'll probably lose our way and actually need them to be heroes, so we might as well recognize them as heroes now. Friends will show up unexpectedly when you are incapable of doing something on your own. They'll bring you home and make sure you're safe and well-fed, physically and spiritually. Make sure they get the recognition they rightfully deserve.

Jesus is a hero. He sacrificed himself willingly to rescue us from our sin and darkness. He came in unexpectedly with a humble entrance to bring us home where we belong. He has a plan of action for us, and that plan of action involves following him faithfully. I guarantee that you'll fail along the way, just like I have many times. Even so, he still comes to redeem us, just as he promises. The champion of the entire world, who died as the true example of a hero, deeply loves us and never leaves us stranded. Even on our islands of anxiety, depression, addiction, or whatever else is on your island, we are not without hope. Because in the distance, coming with haste, is Jesus, speeding towards us with strength, ferocity, and a promise to bring us home.

Chapter 10
BEWARE THE SCARE

This might classify me as a psycho, but I love scary movies. Well, I love the adrenaline rush, maybe not so much the scare. Sometimes the creepy moments can get under my skin, but the excitement and anticipation is what makes them so good. I also think that getting a good scare out of people is one of the funniest things in the world. The reaction on their faces when you jump out and scream is absolutely priceless. I will go to great lengths to get a few seconds of someone screaming, which in turn leads to me not being able to breathe because of laughter.

I've been roommates with my friend Chris for a couple of years now, so living with him I have figured out some of his greatest fears. One of those fears is snakes; he hates them with a burning passion. I haven't taken advantage of this knowledge yet, but I'm sure I will in the future. However, I have learned of other things that scare him. One night, we watched a scary movie that had a particular nun that was, honestly, quite frightening. I ended up both loving and hating the movie because it was so terrifying, but Chris was all hate and no love. He was so wary of me that he began locking his doors frequently every night to make sure I wouldn't jump out and scare him.

Come on now, Chris. I wasn't going to be that obvious. I was going to wait a while and let him forget about it. Then, I would make my move. To be fair, I planned on pulling a prank a couple weeks after we had seen the movie, but I forgot about scaring him. It was months later before I even remembered about the idea. My idea was to replicate exactly what he was afraid of. I went online shopping and found the perfect item: a nun costume! I would just put this on and pop out at him when he least expected it. He would be scarred for life, and I would have a few hearty minutes of laughter. It was a brilliant idea, one that would go down in the history books.

After receiving my nun costume in the mail, I was excited to get the ball rolling. I found a day to execute my plan, and I decided I would get up early in the morning before he did to hide in the bathroom. At 5:30 A.M., my alarm clock went off, and I changed into the costume. I rushed downstairs, and I hid in the bathroom shower to await him. It felt like forever before he finally got up, but I could hear him rustling in his room. I heard the bathroom door open, and my opportunity to strike came. When he was in sight, I jumped out of the shower and yelled gibberish. The look on his face will forever make me laugh. He was so scared that no sound came out of his mouth. His eyes just enlarged double their regular size and he froze like a statue.

Needless to say, he was furious, but he eventually forgave me.

The second time I scared him in the costume (yes, there was a second time – I'm such a good roommate), it was just me and Chris at our apartment. We had both had good days and were in cheerful moods, so I figured this was as good of a time as ever to shock the living daylights out of him. He was in the bathroom, so I knew this was a perfect moment to execute an attack. I rapidly changed into the nun costume and turned off all the lights. I hid behind the island in the kitchen and patiently awaited my prey. When he came into the kitchen, I didn't scream, but kept my head down and sprinted toward him. This time, he jumped and let out a shout like a startled elephant. Unlike my first attempt, I had to run away from him to avoid getting punched. He was rattled for a good five minutes, but he eventually laughed about it and let me off the hook.

I'm able to prank Chris like this not only because we are close friends, but because he is able to forgive. If he didn't forgive me for scaring him, he could become resentful and unwilling to be around me. Time after time, I test his patience to get a laugh, and he still is able to start new with me each time. Chris is like this in more serious matters as well. No matter how much you wrong him or push the wrong buttons, he hastily forgives, and it's like you never did anything at all. With Chris, you can hit the reset button as many times as you want at no cost to you.

Forgiving people is tough, especially when someone does something to you that hurts you deeply. Each one of us is prone to wronging others. We've wronged Jesus countless times, yet he is the perfect example of forgiveness. Everything we have ever done or ever will do that separates us from him, he is willing to push aside to forgive and forget. Every single day is another opportunity for us to start new and put the past behind us. If I had to constantly be forgiving a friend for something they did wrong every day, I would start to get a little annoyed, but Jesus, in his grace and mercy, wipes all our wrongs away and makes them rights. Jesus tells us that if we are willing to confess our sins, then he will be faithful and forgive us.

It's not fun when someone hurts me; it weighs heavily on my heart. I can't even fathom how Jesus feels when the billions of people in the world do things that don't honor him. Many times, people hurt others so bad, that there may never be forgiveness between them, and the relationship is lost. What's so mind-blowing is that we could never do anything that Jesus wouldn't forgive us for. No matter how much it hurts him to see us doing wrong, he leaves our past in the past and gives us a fresh start every single time.

Sometimes, it's even difficult for us to forgive someone once because we feel they have done something so terrible to us. To see how Jesus wants us to forgive, we look to what he says in the book of Matthew. Peter asks Jesus about forgiveness. He asks Jesus how many times we should be

willing to forgive someone who sins against us and questions
if seven times is a good number of times. Jesus answers that
we should not forgive the wrongdoer seven times, but
seventy-seven! That's a lot of times to forgive someone, and
to forgive someone that many times in a row, it would have
to become almost automatic. The point of what Jesus is
saying is not to give us an exact number of times we should
pardon someone, but to tell us that we should keep on
forgiving even though instances may keep happening.

There may be a situation in your life where your mind is
set on not forgiving someone. Your heart has become
hardened and calloused because of the way they treated you
or spoke to you. You may not think you can forgive them on
your own, and you're probably right. However, when you let
Jesus soften you, and you look through his eyes at your
enemies, you'll have an entirely new heart that is focused on
mending open wounds. You'll be able to see them for who
Jesus sees them and understand the full depth of his love and
grace.

Maybe you're going through a situation in your life
where someone didn't do you wrong, but you did them
wrong. That person can't seem to forgive you, and they have
spite toward you. A vital step in mending that broken
relationship is to simply ask for forgiveness for whatever you
may have done. It might take a while for them to have a
change of heart, but you'd be surprised at most outcomes
when you're genuine, lay your heart out on the table for

them, and ask them to have grace with you when you know you screwed up.

Why is asking for forgiveness an important step in mending broken relationships? Because it's what Jesus asks us to do. When we confess to him the wrongs we've done and are truly sorry about the broken conditions of our heart, he is compassionate and wipes the slate clean from all the dirt we put on it. Jesus knows that we're going to mess up time and time again, but he needs us to be conscious of our sins by coming to him and asking for his grace.

Forgiveness is one of the most powerful tools in the world. It can transform lives and repair relationships that seemed too off-the-rails to ever recover. Therefore, we should be kind and show grace with our friends when they wound us either intentionally or unintentionally. Conversely, we need to be ahead of the game when it comes to realizing our wrongdoings, being genuine in our apologies, and asking for grace. Become a friend who doesn't even think twice about forgiving, realize wrongdoing as a human mistake, and move on.

Being forgiven doesn't mean that you get to keep doing what you've been doing. Being genuinely apologetic means that your heart will enter a state of repentance. If you've wronged someone, why would you want to keep hurting them over and over? Being forgiven means that there is an expectation for you to have a change of heart even though they'll forgive you if you wrong them again. Jesus wants us to take steps towards righteousness, but he will show grace to us even when we wrong him again.

Chris is forgiving when I wrong him, which is something I'm truly grateful for. He doesn't hold grudges, and he wants to solve a problem immediately once it arises. Of course, I always do my best to change myself when I have wronged Chris. However, being repentant doesn't apply to pranking, especially when he knows it's in good fun. So with that said, Chris, beware the scare. I'm coming for you.

Chapter 11
SURI

I must admit there are some truly exotic foods in the world, although "exotic" could mean really good or really bad. There are delicate and decadent dishes that are fit for royalty. There are also seemingly disgusting meals that are a normal part of other cultures. Sometimes I think that foreign locals get tourists to try disgusting foods just to get a good laugh and see the tourists' reactions. "Stupid tourists," they think, "they'll try anything". I used to watch Fear Factor all the time as a kid and was amazed at the kinds of things people would eat. There were roaches, spiders, and all kinds of quirky bugs I would never think of eating.

Little did I know I would be eating some crazy things like the Fear Factor contestants did, as I have tried some outlandish "food" on my trips outside the United States. I never thought I would have the guts to eat some of them, but here I am saying I have. I've eaten food like alpaca (rest in peace, I'm sorry) and a piece of guinea pig (NEVER AGAIN). But perhaps one of the most gut-wrenching things I've eaten comes from one of my trips to Peru. The Peruvians call it "suri".

SURI

What exactly is suri? It's a worm. Yes, you read that right – a worm. Disgusting, I know. Apparently, this isn't any regular worm, so let me tell you a little about it. Suri is considered a delicacy in Peru (I'm thinking the same thing – how can a worm be a delicacy?). Historically, it has been consumed by the indigenous people in the Amazon where it's pulled off a common tree called the Aguaje. I had never heard of suri before I tried it, but after reading about it, evidently tourists are eager to try it. A lot of people also think it tastes good; some say it is sweet and rich in flavor. One way to cook it is skewer style, like a kabob, over coals for a few minutes, which is how we tasted it.

When we first went by a market stand and were instructed to try them by our trip leader, I thought he was joking. There was absolutely zero desire in me to remotely put that near my face, but for some reason I didn't want to deny myself the opportunity to be adventurous and try something absurd. Along with my friends Jeremiah and Reagan, I was handed a stick full of suri worms. Our eyes flickered between the worms and each other, silently agreeing that this could possibly be the worst decision we would ever make. We were all freaking out at first, wondering how we could possibly stomach this. We made the decision that we should probably eat it at the same time, so no one would chicken out if someone had a bad reaction.

On the count of three, we popped the worms into our mouths. I made my mouth as hollow as possible to avoid sloshing it around, and I took my bite. Immediately, I felt the crunch in my mouth, and the slimy juice exploded onto my inner cheek. Through a couple of gags, I managed to swallow the suri. I could feel the crunchy shell scratching the inside of my throat as it slowly slid down into my stomach. On the contrary to what my research online says, I thought this was disgusting.

I stuck my tongue out to get any remainder of the worm off my tongue while Reagan was gagging with tears in her eyes. But Jeremiah was even more appalled. He started to yell about how disgusting it was and almost threw up. The people at the stand were looking at him, and our youth pastor told him that he might be offending them. So Reagan and I said, "Yeah, you offended them, so you should probably eat another one and act like you liked it." Either Jeremiah was deeply empathetic to their culture, or we did an exceptional job of convincing him, but he reluctantly agreed to eat another. I watched in horror as he popped another one in his mouth with a grimace on his face. He chewed with his soul distressed and looked at the people shouting, "Yum! This is really good!" I couldn't help but laugh at his apparent distress.

I felt sorry for Jeremiah because he had to stomach another one of those filthy creatures. The fact of the matter is, it could have been me or Reagan who had to eat another. We were just as sickened, but Jeremiah took all the heat for potentially offending their culture. He could have made us eat another with him. Instead, he solely faced the battle by himself in our place. He faced the pain and discomfort of another "delicacy," so we wouldn't have to do it again to make up for our offense to their culture.

If Jesus was physically on Earth with us again and was in that moment, he would have taken my place just like Jeremiah did. In fact, he probably would have eaten the whole kebab. Jesus is more than willing to pick up our slack and take all the blame. He took all the blame for us when he was hung on the cross – all the blame for our past, present, and future. He faced the battle of sin completely by himself, taking the weight of the world upon his shoulders. He died so that we wouldn't have to make up for our transgressions any longer.

What Jeremiah did for us is he took the weight and pressure off our shoulders about having to eating another worm and placed it on himself. A verse that demonstrates this concept beautifully and simply is Galatians 6:2. It says, "Bear one another's burdens, and so fulfill the law of Christ." The phrase "bear one another's burdens" is one of the most striking things for me to think about. Visually, I think about someone carrying something extremely heavy, being so weighed down that they can't walk. Then someone comes along and lifts all of that weight off their friend's shoulders. There's a sigh of relief and an immediate liberation as the friend is now free of their struggle because of the other person's sacrifice.

While I was doing my research on suri, I learned that in these worms, along with other nutrients, there is a rich source of iron. Our body needs the component of iron in our hemoglobin to carry oxygen from our lungs and transport it through our bodies. This important nutrient we need to survive is found in these worms. Of course, there are also other iron-rich foods that we can eat, but I didn't think it was a coincidence that these worms were heavy in iron. Jeremiah bearing that burden of those iron-rich worms was a way to sharpen and deepen our friendship.

A lot of things happen to us in life that cause a lot of pain and force us to do some heavy lifting. Often, it's our thoughts that weigh us down, and we keep thinking about all the negative things a situation brings us. It drains us, takes all of our energy, and we're left feeling endlessly tired. Jesus invites us to come to him so that he can take that burden from us and replenish our lives. He says all who are weary, exhausted, and burdened will find rest in him.

This offer for rest isn't a one-time offer or a single-use coupon. This invitation from Jesus applies for the rest of our lives on Earth and for eternity. Isaiah 46:4 says, "Even to your old age and gray hairs I am he, I am he who will sustain you. I have made you and I will carry you; I will sustain you and I will rescue you." No situation is too heavy for Jesus to handle. You may think that no one could possibly help you free yourself from the chains that are holding you down, but through every second, Jesus is there to provide freedom. You are his creation, and he made you just the way you were supposed to be. When the load is too heavy to bear and you fall down, he'll pick you and your burdens up to carry. Jesus has a lot of endurance, and he's more than capable of picking up the heaviness on your back.

Seeing the best in your friends and watching them flourish is a reward in itself. Friends stick together, and they don't let each other be crushed by the weight of the world. If your friend had a backpack full of one hundred pounds, and you only had ten, wouldn't you want to take some of their weight and put it in yours? No one likes to see their friends struggle, especially when it's something that's eating them alive. In order for our friends to flourish, sometimes we have to sacrifice some of our own comfort.

What does bearing each other's burdens look like, exactly? The truth is, there's no practical, one-size-fits-all, easy answer. Everyone is different, and we each have our own personalities, so it varies from person to person. However, a universal method is listening. Every person wants to be listened to, to have a voice, and to know their emotions matter. A burden can become heavy because it's bottled up and keeps growing, adding more negative thoughts that turn into habitual nuisances. Releasing those thoughts can help, however small, in getting rid of some of that load. As selfish humans, we are prone to hearing the words that come out of someone else's mouth and thinking of our next response. But how often do we actually listen? How often do we take someone else's thoughts and feelings to heart and process them? Are we really listening, or are we just searching for a way to point the conversation back to us?

Friends are burden-bearers, and sometimes the burdens can be extreme and something none of us want to carry, like that gut-wrenching suri that Jeremiah swallowed for us. Friends are willing to go through any situation, no matter how difficult or disgusting, in order to see joy on a loved one's face. Even if it was partly another person's burden, they are willing to take it all. Jesus wants to carry your burden, so let him. He stood in the way for your burdens so that you could have abundant life. Be that example when your friends are struggling. Whether it's listening or being empathetic through your actions, seize that burden with willingness so that your friends will be overflowing with exuberant joy and fervent love.

Chapter 12

DON THE DENTIST

I've never understood all the negative buzz around dentists' offices. Sure, I get a little nervous that something is going to be wrong with my teeth, but I'm not scared of the dentist because I know they're only trying to help me clean my teeth and make them healthy. There are times when I'm uncomfortable because I don't like the feeling of my teeth being scraped, but they're just doing their job. The most amazing dentist I have ever met is Don - Don the Dentist. What a glorious name for a dentist. I met Don on a medical mission trip to Honduras where I got to watch him closely and learn a little about dentistry.

On our second day in Honduras, I was asked to be a dental assistant for Don. I had no prior qualifications, but I did feel a little prideful that I got to work alongside a qualified professional. Of course, I didn't need any prior qualifications as the work mostly consisted of cleaning tools, writing simple prescriptions, and holding a spit bucket. Even though my job wasn't the most glorious, I still had a blast learning from Don and observe him doing his handiwork.

The word of the medical center we set up must have spread around town fairly well, because there were lines and rows of chairs full of people waiting to be checked out. I watched Don perform many operations throughout the day. He operated on the young, old, and everyone in between. It didn't matter where they had come from; Don was going to see everyone and make sure their teeth were in top shape. Unfortunately, to get their teeth in top shape, this meant that Don had to pull quite a few teeth that had cavities or were rotting.

The majority of the procedures went well. Don would check their mouths, clean them, and they would most likely have to get a tooth or two pulled. However, there were a couple of procedures that had a few complications. One of these complications was an eighteen-year-old girl that he had to work an entire hour on. He didn't have the proper tools for a speedy procedure, so he had to operate with what he had. You could tell she was a little bit scared, so we held her hand during most of the process. Don meticulously worked on her tooth little by little, and finally to our relief, he removed all the pieces of tooth.

Another memorable complication was one that was harder to watch. This man had a few teeth that had cavities, infected areas, and were rotting. Naturally, this wasn't going to be a fun process. With this patient, I was holding the spit bucket so he could get rid of excess saliva and any blood that may have entered the mouth as a result of the procedure. I can't remember if there was numbing medicine or not, but I remember watching him and cringing because of the amount of pain he was experiencing. A few times he would yell in pain, and I could see the tears welling up in his eyes. I think one time he attempted to get up, but they had to convince him to stay and finish the operation. I couldn't even imagine the discomfort he was going through, but as Don finished working on the man, I could see a sense of comfort in his eyes knowing that he had been healed and would be free of pain after a couple weeks of recovery.

Patient by patient, Don worked tirelessly to make sure every person's teeth were healthy. It wasn't glamorous work by any means. Don had to constantly work with cavities and infections that produced blood and saliva. I had to hold the collection bucket and clean tools, not to mention the pungent alcohol smell that we cleaned the tools with. Even though it wasn't a glitzy job, it was well worth seeing the faces after the procedure when they knew they would be in good health soon.

Don was like a healing machine, working through one person in need after another. If someone came in to have their teeth fixed, they were going to have them fixed, no questions asked. A lot of procedures were painless; they went in and had a pleasant experience with their visit. However, a few people were filled with fear and distress after they had teeth removed. Likely, they would also be feeling pain for a few weeks until the wound was completely cured. Even though there was extreme pain in some cases, Don knew he had to cause this pain in order for the pain to disappear in the future.

Physical healing is an extraordinary process. Our bodies work tirelessly, sending cells to injured parts of our bodies to make new flesh and restore us. I would venture to say that inner healing is even more extraordinary. When we're hurt by the afflictions of life, sometimes the recovery process is quick and painless. We can forget about something easily and excitedly jump out of bed in the morning. For deeper wounds, this process isn't as straightforward. It takes time to recuperate, and the mending of the wounds can sometimes hurt worse than the affliction itself.

It's a tough thing to swallow, but sometimes it's really going to hurt when you're trying to heal. The pain and suffering can seem unbearable and like the whole world is crushing in around you from every side. You may have sleepless nights, be drained of energy, and be devoid of any motivation for the things you love in life. The good news is, Jesus is working in you and mending the broken things in you. The pain is only temporary, but Jesus is eternal. He comes to restore, to renew, and to redeem all of our shattered pieces.

While Jesus was on Earth, he did a lot of healing. He healed the sick, the blind, the diseased, and more. When he walked the Earth, he never turned anyone down to be healed. In fact, he sought out the ones who didn't come to him because they thought they couldn't be healed. He was so good at it that a woman touched his robe and she was instantly healed of her illness. That's an extraordinary amount of power! Why don't we believe that Jesus can do the same for us? We think that our wounds are too great for him to heal, but we're terribly mistaken. When you ask for healing, he will restore you when you come to him.

The reason this healing is possible now is because of Jesus's death on the cross for us and his injuries in the place of ours. By his wounds, we're able to be healed. Our bodies are submerged in brokenness and weakness, but one day, they will be raised and made new in strength and glory. No person is too far in depravity for Jesus to shine his loving light upon them. Jesus is here to comfort us, to fill in the holes left in us, and to give us life.

Although Don didn't have the right tools to work on the eighteen-year-old girl's teeth, he still got the job done. Jesus always has the right tools to fix us no matter what situation we're in. He's the best doctor in town, and he always has the handy utensils he needs to get the job done. He is able to heal all broken hearts and bind up wounds routinely. We are his patients, made exactly the way he wanted us to be under his intensive care.

A good doctor we can have in a time of trouble is a friend who heals like Jesus does. Jesus is like the main doctor, and our friends are like the assistants, and it's the assistants who prepare us so that the doctor can come in and do his handiwork. To be healers to our friends, we need to realize that some situations are going to take more than an hour or two to fix. Healing in people can last for years, so it's important to not get discouraged if we aren't seeing immediate results. As healing assistants, it's our job to make sure that our friends are receiving proper care and attention so that when Jesus comes in, our friends are primed for him to stitch us up.

Another important thing to realize is that the work we're going to be doing for our friends while they heal isn't all glamourous. You have to do the dirty work, watch them spit out unwanted things from their life, and watch as your friends endure unfathomable ache and hurt. There might be moments when they want to get up and walk away because they think their condition before is better than the pain they're experiencing now, but we have to convince them to stay and finish because there's so much joy after the pain.

When we work out our muscles, the fibers tear and cause us to be sore. However, after our soreness, the damaged fibers are fused, and new strands are created. They increase in thickness and make our muscles grow. Our new and improved muscles make us stronger, more resilient, and able to carry more weight. The same is true of our inner healing. Recovering from a devastating situation shapes our character to be stronger the next time we encounter a similar situation. We'll be more resilient and apt to let Jesus handle the situation instead of trying to handle it on our own.

Sharpening friends by taking the role of a healer means that we need to prime their hearts for Jesus to work. We're only human, and we can only do so much to sew up their cuts. By loving in the way that Jesus loves and doing the dirty work, we get to prepare their hearts for Jesus to move in them. Our friends should have an immediate pass to get into our "doctor's office," just like we have an immediate pass to speak with Jesus – anytime, anywhere.

We don't need any prior qualifications to seam up our friends. We don't need a magic formula, special training, or any philosophical words to say. Jesus invites us to come as we are. We should come to help our friends just as we are and meet our friends where they are. We don't need to have all the answers or a perfect strategy in healing our friends. All we need is a heart devoted to being a servant and an expectation that Jesus will restore and heal.

Chapter 13
A SALSA CRISIS

Science and anatomy tell us that what flows through our veins is blood. I'm here to tell you that's not what flows through mine at all. What flows through mine is salsa. If I was dropped off on an island and only had one food item in which to survive, it would be salsa. I don't know if it's the Texan in me, or if it's the fact that all my mom ate while I was in the womb was Tex-Mex, but you can never go wrong chips and salsa. My parents used to buy me unreasonably large jars of it so I wouldn't eat the entire thing in a day, but really that didn't slow me down.

During a spring break trip to Colorado, I encountered a bit of a "problem" with salsa. We had just been through a long, tiring day full of hiking, adventuring, and exploring, and our friend group was going back to Lindsey's grandparents' house. Lindsey's grandparents were so kind to us and usually had food waiting on the table for us when we returned. This time, we were awaited by a giant bowl of chips and salsa. Now, there was no actual problem with the taste of salsa. In fact, I don't think I've ever eaten salsa that I didn't like. It's what we did with the salsa that was the problem.

Everyone was exhausted from the day's activities, and quite frankly, we were feeling really gross. All my other friends decided to go ahead and take showers before dinner, but my friend Katie and I were too enthralled by the salsa and let everyone else shower first. We sat down at the table and marveled at the glorious sight in front of us. It was perfect to fulfill a hungry, exhausted stomach. The lightly salted chips with the smooth salsa complemented each other with such exquisite satisfaction.

It started out as a casual conversation with Katie talking about our day and munching on our snack. However, the delicious flavor overtook us, and we started devouring the salsa like savages. Katie would take a large scoop, and I would immediately sweep in after. It was an endless, vicious cycle, and our supply began to run low. But who could blame us? It was a worthy snack to quench our hunger after such an active day. As the salsa began to diminish, Katie and I looked at each other.

"We should probably save some for everyone else, right?" Katie asked.

"Yeah, we should!" I responded as I kept funneling salsa into my mouth.

"Just one more," Katie replied.

We all know how "just one more" goes. One more led into twenty more, and our reserves were almost depleted. Neither of us wanted the other to be the last one to taste the mouthwatering mixture. I was concerned about the others getting to have some, but I was apparently more concerned with how much I could fit into my own stomach. Eventually, Jack joined us near the final life of the salsa and helped us eat. Within minutes, all of the salsa was gone. All that was in front of us was now empty, a desolate fragment of the past.

Katie and I looked at each other half in disbelief, half in pride. We had officially entered crisis mode. While everyone else was in the shower, we managed to go through every last bit of the chips and salsa. Should we hide it? Should we tell them we ate it all? If we told them, they would probably get mad at us, and we would have to sit in shame knowing we deprived them of one of the best foods to ever exist. After a little deliberation, we leaned towards not telling them. However, if we kept it secret, it would be on our conscience, wouldn't be honest, and would probably come forward within the hour anyway.

In the midst of our crisis, we were met by Lindsey's grandmother. She approached us and looked at the aftermath of our savagery.

"Oh, are we all out? Let me get the rest of it for you," she remarked.

Our eyes instantly lit up, and tight smiles creeped across our faces. We were saved! We didn't have to worry that we would anger everyone else. We didn't have to keep secrets or hide our greedy actions. We got an entire fill of chips and salsa, yet there was still more to be dispersed. It was a true miracle. Lindsey's grandmother came out with another round of salsa, and my heart skipped a beat. We were both so tempted to keep eating it, but we forced ourselves to refrain as we had already been greedy enough to eat the entire other bowl.

Finally, the others came out for dinner, and we smiled like nothing had ever happened. Eventually, we told them what happened, and everything was fine, mainly because there was an extra serving of salsa. Lindsey's grandmother had rescued us from certain trouble, and we all ate the new batch of chips and salsa in harmony.

Katie and I were greedy when it came to that snack, but we ended up being provided for in the end. Katie didn't judge me for continuing to eat, and I didn't judge her, but we should have made the conscious decision to stop. If it weren't for Lindsey's grandmother, we would have been in a pretty awkward situation. However, now that we've looked at the situation in retrospect, we knew that we should have provided for our friends. Katie taught me that my needs are not the most important.

Selfishness and greediness can effortlessly take over us, and we end up taking away the opportunity for someone else to be blessed. We take too much, and we're left having nothing for ourselves or for anyone else. When we abide in Jesus, we will never be left with emptiness. He will provide for us more than anything we could ever ask for. He will replenish us and keep on replenishing us, like an endless supply of salsa. When we're empty, he checks right in with us and refills us abundantly.

Once you get a taste of his love, you'll never want to stop receiving it. Yes, it's even better than this salsa was. You never have to worry about running out of his love; he'll always come back with another round. No matter how much our hands keep taking, he faithfully gives us what we need.

Jesus already knows our needs and will provide for them, but he wants us to talk to him about our needs so that we can grow our relationship and become dependent upon him. When we ask of him in prayer and have faith, we will receive. Prayer is a conversation with Jesus and should be honest and completely open. When Jesus sees the honesty and purity of our hearts, he will give to us our inner desires.

It might be hard to see how Jesus is providing for you sometimes, but if you sit down and think about it, he's probably provided for you more than you give him credit for. In a story from 1 Kings, a drought falls upon the land, and God tells a man named Elijah to go to a brook to drink water, and he makes ravens supply Elijah with food. It's kind of a weird thing to think about. Elijah just looked up to the sky during his regular routine, and said, "Oh look, there's the ravens with my food." God provided for Elijah in an unconventional, unexpected, and weird method. If you're having trouble thinking of how Jesus has provided for you, you're probably not looking in the right places. Jesus will show up in the most unexpected ways to provide for our needs, and some of those provisions we may have not realized were needed.

When we become complacent and comfortable with our friendships, we can end up taking a lot more than we should. Instead of being the providers, we become the deprivers. We've all taken more than our fair share from a friendship before, and it's likely that you're overflowing with things to provide for your friends. To provide means to supply or to equip someone with something necessary. Not only do we supply our friends with needs, but we equip them. We give them the tools they need in order to be prepared for whatever life throws at them. Providing isn't simply about giving, it's about giving with in an intent to build.

Providing isn't just about physical things, either. You can provide all of the material things in the world, but in the end, an empty person who was filled with material items will be left just as empty as when they started. Providing is about love. If you want to know what kind of love you should provide, check out 1 Corinthians 13:4-7. "Love is patient, love is kind. It does not envy, it does not boast, it is not proud. It does not dishonor others, it is not self-seeking, it is not easily angered, it keeps no record of wrongs. Love does not delight in evil but rejoices with the truth. It always protects, always trusts, always hopes, always perseveres."

At first, this may seem like a laundry list of items or a checklist you need to complete. However, love isn't about a checklist. When you live your life focused on love, all these pieces will fall into place naturally. Be humble in the way that you provide to others. Have a gentle spirit and protect your friends from harm. Give them hope, because it's what we cling to in our desperation, and persevere because perseverance is what fuels our hope.

Jesus provides us an eternal supply of love and everything else we could ever ask for. With him, you'll never be empty; he fills our cups until they're overflowing and we don't know what to do with ourselves. When you don't know what to do with that overflow, pour it into someone else's cup. Provide for them like Jesus provides for us. Equip them with tools to be able to love unconditionally. Without equipping them, they might have a harder time getting the tools to sharpen others. Sharpen your friends so they can sharpen others. Most of all, let Jesus be the center of where we place our hope, knowing that he will always provide.

Chapter 14
DON'T ROB ME OF A BLESSING

Grandparents are truly some of the most remarkable people in this world. People always say that grandparents are the ones who spoil children, and I think they really take this to heart. From all the little gifts, hugs and kisses, and warm cookies, grandparents have a knack for turning a pure heart rotten (in the best way, of course). They're never inconsistent in spoiling you. Each time you enter through their front door, they smother you in love and affection and make sure you're fat and happy.

Sorry to break the news, but my grandparents are the best in the world. Maybe that's my rotten heart talking, but my Nana and Poppy are some of the most compassionate people I know. They got married at an early age, and Poppy began a ministry that he would stay committed to until this very day. They have been to so many countries sharing the love of Christ, that Poppy literally forgot the number and names of all of them. They've spoiled not only me, but thousands of people around the world.

I'm pretty sure that my Nana got her tendency to pamper grandkids from her mom. My great-grandmother, Nane as we called her, was also remarkable. We would go over to her house, and she would have Skip-Bo set up for us, along with chocolate chip cookies and milk. She was sweet, kind, and always made sure we left her house with something in our hand. Every time we left, it was a dollar bill and a Rice Krispies treat to hold us over until next time.

When I go into my grandparents' house, it automatically feels like I'm safe and at home. There's warmth and tenderness in the atmosphere, allowing me to feel relaxed and protected. Whatever the magic is that's in the air blocks out all the rest of life's worries and gives me space to just breathe for a moment. What's awesome about my grandparents is that they're more undisciplined than all of us grandkids combined. This creates space for me to be myself, and I can look up to them both as my grandparents and as friends.

Just like my Nane, my grandparents refuse to let me leave the house without something, whether that's food, money, hugs, or something else that will ruin me entirely. There's no use in refusing because they will have it their way if it's the last thing they do. A tactic that Nana likes to use is to get a stern look on her face (although I know she's not capable of anything remotely stern) and say the phrase, "Don't rob me of a blessing!" Whoa, whoa, whoa. Slam on the brakes here. As a grandkid, that's completely unfair, and she's definitely using guilt trip to her advantage. How would

I justify "robbing" my own grandmother? That's right, I can't. There's no good explanation. Automatically, she has the upper hand.

I've tried to fight her on that phrase before, and know I know that it's pointless to even try. I've tried to reason that they could use what they were giving me for other people. Against my efforts, Poppy would chime in and also become somber, explaining that they wanted to do something nice for me, and that they didn't want to miss on the opportunity to do so. After thinking about that, I agree with them. If I tried to do something out of the kindness of my heart and someone refused, it would hurt me a little bit knowing that I couldn't see them have joy even though I desired to.

What Nana and Poppy tell me each time they pour out love, gifts, meals, hugs, laughter, a safe space, and countless other things from their big hearts is that it's a free gift. I don't have to do anything to earn it, and I don't have to work for it. It's simply there for the taking. All I have to do is accept their gifts with a grateful heart. They aren't giving it to me in return for anything I did. In fact, they don't even want anything in return for their outpouring of love.

How many times have you caught yourself doing this in your faith? I know I think this way too often. We try to earn our place with Jesus by performance or actions that justify why we deserve his grace. The reality is, we don't deserve anything at all. No amount of good deeds could ever earn us a spot in the kingdom of Heaven. We're held back from accepting this notion of a free gift because our minds our trained to think in terms of actions. To get good grades, you have to earn them. To get money for a living, you have to earn it. To get that promotion, you have to earn it. Nearly everything in our lives is based on action in exchange for something we want.

In a total flip of everything we know, Jesus comes in and tells us that we don't have to earn anything he's offering us. He wants us to accept his gift to us. His love? Free. His mercy? Free. His grace? Free. His invitation for us to live eternally with him? Absolutely free, no price tag, no hidden fees! Jesus's gift to us is unconditional love for an eternity and continual forgiveness every time we mess up.

Romans 6:23 says, "For the wages of sin is death, but the gift of God is eternal life through Christ Jesus our Lord." Other translations also include the word free in front of 'gift'. A wage is a regular payment to someone. Our wage for our sin was ultimately death, but it was paid for by Jesus's death on the cross. We owed him so much that the only solution was for us to die. But instead, he offered a free gift to us. He invites us into eternal life with him. There's no fine print, no charge, and no surprises. The only surprise is that someone would be willing to give a gift to us of that proportion, asking nothing in exchange.

A true friend won't need anything in return for love. Love is offered with the intent of wanting nothing in exchange. That means there's nothing you could ever say or do that would make your friends love you any less. The same thing applies to us loving our friends. Even if someone does something so terrible and heartbreaking to you, Jesus calls us to love them still. Nothing they could ever say, do, or think should ever change the way you love them. When they ask for forgiveness, it should be freely given. Love is not redeemed by actions or favors. Love is not measured by the amount of our good deeds, but it measured by our willingness to provide undying grace and receive mercy with a repentant heart.

The question is: How willing are you to give perpetual grace? Will you still pump out grace even when someone pushes you over the edge? Will your heart be keen enough to look at them with empathetic eyes? I bet you have a boundary in mind, just like we all do. I bet you're thinking, "If someone did this to me, then it would take a lot for them to earn my love and trust back." SOUND THE ALARM, BECAUSE YOU JUST SAID IT! You just said the word that shouldn't coexist with love: 'earn'. Love is never earned; it is extended with open arms out of the compassion of our hearts, regardless of how deep someone wounds us. Loving with grace means that even when someone pushes you over the edge, your heart is willing to fly back to where they pushed you, let go of your anger, and offer nothing but a chance for reconciliation.

It's easier said than done, I know. How can we love them in that way? What if they're just so annoying, offensive, or unpleasant to be around? What if they did something to you that your heart just can't seem to forgive? The reality is, most of the time, we're not able to love in that way on our own. However, when we can't, Jesus can. We have to open our hearts up to him and say, "Jesus, show your love through me because I can't do it on my own. Let my heart forgive as you forgive me. Let my spirit be full of grace and gentleness, and let me extend it enduringly." Once you depend on him to show loving grace in that way and realize the extent of his free gift towards us, then allowing him to work in our hearts makes loving people a whole lot easier.

When we spend time with our friends, they should never leave feeling empty. They should always leave feeling fulfilled and taking something edifying from us we offer for free. This doesn't mean that you can't sit on the couch together and binge watch a couple episodes of your favorite TV shows. Even I like to do that. It means that your friends should leave that binge watching session knowing that you sit down with them with the intent to build upon your friendship. If your friend leaves with that fulfillment, then you've offered them the right thing.

An issue with our hearts in receiving Jesus's free gift is that we don't think we're good enough for it. That couldn't be farther from the truth. Jesus's invite to eternal life is to everyone who is willing to accept it, and the reason he extends it is because he says we are good enough. This thought that separates us from seeing the truth goes back to our notion of deserving. If we really got what we deserved, it would be a trillion times worse than what Jesus is gifting us. We don't deserve his gift, but that's the whole point. We don't deserve it, yet it's ours for the taking.

Our responsibility to our friends is to recreate that magic in the air that exists in my Nana and Poppy's house. The funny thing is, it's not even a mysterious magic. The way the magic in the atmosphere surges to life is because of how we live. If we live our lives eager to offer our love freely in the same manner that Christ does to us, all the pieces will fall into place. People will be around you and notice something different. They won't be able to pinpoint what it is, but you know exactly what the magic is: the unfathomable love of Jesus.

I used to be frustrated with Nana and Poppy when they would stubbornly make me take whatever they were offering. I would feel irritated when they would say, "You have to take it, or you're going to rob us of a blessing." Now I know exactly why they use that phrase. Jesus is offering us something far better than we could ever find from this Earth. Don't rob him of that blessing. He paid a pretty heavy price for that blessing. Plus, it doesn't cost you anything. All you have to do is confess that you don't deserve it because of your sin, take it with a repentant heart, and say 'yes'! I don't know of any better bargain.

Amusingly, I get to use "don't rob me of a blessing" on my grandparents when I want to do something nice for them, so it kind of backfired that they introduced me to this phrase in the first place. As funny as it is, they taught me a valuable lesson from it. Our friends need us to be dishing out love to them free of charge. Not only do our friends need it, but the whole world needs it. Wouldn't it be amazing to be so plentiful giving love that you forgot how many people and nations you gave it to? I could only dream of making that sort of an impact. To make that impact, it starts with the conditions of our heart. It takes knowing the full extent of the invitation into the Kingdom and passion to share it with others. It takes us opening our hands to the world, expecting nothing in return.

Chapter 15

PUMPING IRON

I never believed in the "Freshman Fifteen". I thought I was active enough that I would be totally fine, and I would stay the exact same weight. Against all my initial beliefs, the Freshman Fifteen showed itself to be anything but a myth. The buffet near my dorm didn't help my case either. In my final year in college, I decided that I wanted my body to be healthier. I wasn't at an unhealthy weight by any means, but I wanted to challenge myself to be stronger and be proud of the work I put in to my body, achieving a healthier status.

The main way I wanted to become healthier is by becoming stronger. I wanted to lift weights so that my body would be used to using all the muscles, I would feel good, and I would be confident in my abilities. However, I didn't want to go to the gym alone because I had insecurities and hate when people watch me exercise. Cue the person I asked to go to the gym with me: Brady.

Brady had recently become our new roommate, and he was perfect to go with me because he's the fittest person I know. Brady is strong on both the outside and the inside. His strength shows in the gym and in his character. I've never seen anyone as kind, gentle, and loving as he is. He is patient with people and always wants to help whenever we can. When we moved in with Brady, he helped us do everything, even when he didn't have to. He carried our belongings, helped us assemble our furniture, and made sure we had everything we needed. He was also able to encourage me while I was trying to build my physical strength.

The first time he came to the gym with me, I won't lie, I was nervous. Brady is a muscular human, and I wasn't sure what I was in for. When we got into the gym, he started explaining what we were going to do in our workout and asked me if I knew what certain exercises were. Of course I didn't know what he wasn't talking about; it had been years since I intentionally exercised. I listened in bewilderment as he explained everything, and I had to watch him do it first before I knew what to do.

After our warmup, it was time for "the real deal". Before I came with him, I had been using the machines, but our workout was apparently just going to consist of dumbbells. How hard could this be? Being my first workout with him, he decided to focus training me on arms. This was what I thought I was best at, so this was going to be a piece of cake. I'd be pumping this iron like nobody's business.

It turns out, I'm much weaker than my ego gives me credit for. It was more intense than any workout I've ever done. In reality, it probably wasn't that bad, but for not exercising regularly in years, it was a doozy. Now I know why Brady is so strong, because he does these exercises I've never heard of that utilize every inch of muscle you have. There was one routine we did where you lay on a bench and slowly let the dumbbells fall behind your head. That one hurt more than any of the others. When I lowered my elbows, I could feel my muscle fibers ripping. I probably looked like a wimp, as I was doing twenty pound dumbbells as opposed to Brady's sixty pound ones.

The lifting we did was so difficult for me that I actually had to reduce the heaviness of what I was lifting. As the hour went by, it was getting really hard to lift my arms up. Even through my feeble attempts, Brady fed encouragement to me and told me to push through. It was never an annoying scream like trainers do, yelling, "Come on, you're not going to get any stronger just sitting there! You've got one more, keep going!" Instead, it was a calm tone, one that truly believed that I could do it, saying, "Don't give up, you've got this." A positive tone and words of affirmation like that motivated me more than someone screaming in my face ever could have.

My arms hurt for an entire week after that. They were tight and hard to move. One time, I even had to roll myself out of bed because I couldn't push myself up. It wasn't a surprise anymore that Brady was so strong because this training he introduced to me really made me feel where my muscles were rebuilding. It didn't stop there, either. My legs felt even worse when we exercised those muscles. Even through the soreness, I knew that was the feeling of becoming stronger.

What's unique about Brady is that he is dually strong and gentle inside and out. He's physically strong but never flaunts it. His character is strong with sincerity, and he shows this through his kind spirit. His personality is ideal for cultivating meaningful relationships with others because of his genuine desire to deeply know people. When Jesus was here on Earth, he also displayed this uniqueness. He was human, but he still had all the power of God. He could have made everyone bow before his feet, but he didn't. Instead, he showed us what kind of king he is by channeling that power to a soft but mighty love.

When I was lifting with Brady, I knew I was weak, and I constantly let him know that I wouldn't be able to go to the extent that he was. When we admit our weaknesses, that's where real change happens. That's when we realize that we're not strong enough on our own. We need someone else to train us so that we can become stronger.

Jesus tells us that his power is made perfect in our weaknesses. When we are frail, broken, and admit that we aren't sufficient alone, he comes in and fills in all the gaps missing in us. The whole premise of his power is that when we are deprived of hope and have run out of steam, he transforms our feebleness into refined strength.

The Bible is full of wisdom about God's strength. Isaiah 40:29-31 states, "He gives strength to the weary and increases the power of the weak. Even youths grow tired and weary, and young men stumble and fall; but those who hope in the Lord will renew their strength. They will soar on wings like eagles; they will run and not grow weary, they will walk and not be faint." To me, this verse sounds a lot like freedom. I love that imagery of being able to fly and run unceasingly without ever being tired or tied down to anything. You're not tied down to your mistakes, failures, addictions, thoughts, or depression. Running like that and sprouting some wings to take flight seems like something you would see in a superhero trailer, but Jesus's strength is much greater than any superhero's.

When I'm knocked down and weak, I have a tendency to question Jesus. I ask how he could allow me to be struggling even though he wants to see me thrive. My gut reaction is to immediately place the blame on him. It isn't until later that I begin considering why I'm struggling. The whole purpose of working out is to build and increase the strength of muscle. Without any resistance and struggle from the muscle, there wouldn't be any progress. Maybe Jesus is teaching us how to be stronger; maybe he's training us to build character in every trial that we face.

Brady doesn't just pump iron in the gym; he pumps spiritual iron into everyone he meets. He's a goldmine for filling people with the essential substances of friendship. He practically breathes the stuff. He's always shoveling out compassion, empathy, integrity, loyalty, unconditional love, generosity, and pretty much any other ingredient you can think of. This is how Jesus teaches us to live: pumping iron like it's all you know how to do.

Coming to Jesus with an intent to be strengthened can cause nervousness. You're afraid that he'll see your weaknesses and look down on you because of your struggles. You're fearful because you don't know what his plan of action is to strengthen you, and you don't want to know the future because you're scared it won't be what you want. Whatever workout plan Jesus has for you, there's no reason for you to be afraid. He's not one of those gym rats who flaunts their strength and judges the weaker ones. His plan is to help you, not to harm you.

When you first get a glimpse of his plan, you might be confused about it and not know what he's talking about. You may not know how to execute the tasks he gives you, but you're not meant to do them on your own. With Jesus as our trainer, we can look to him before we start. If you start before he shows you how, he'll be there beside you to correct you. However, following his plan isn't always an easy routine, and you may not be strong enough to lift a lot of weight at first. When following him, there may be some soreness and pain as a result of your efforts, but this pain doesn't last. You'll get accustomed to pumping the iron, it will become second nature, and you'll be stronger than ever before.

No one ever said the choice to follow Jesus would be an easy one. There might be those people like the gym rats who discourage you and look down upon you. Instead of being fearful of your opposition, be content in your weaknesses. 2 Corinthians 12:10 articulates, "That is why, for Christ's sake, I delight in weaknesses, in insults, in hardships, in persecutions, in difficulties. For when I am weak, then I am strong." That's such a powerful notion to grasp, that being weak makes us strong; it contradicts the basic laws of nature. Survival of the fittest says only the strongest survive to go on. If that's true, then in Jesus's Kingdom, the weak will prosper.

Friends are made to be strong for each other, to train each other, and to pump as much spiritual iron into each other as possible. We're called to be both gentle and strong inside and out. Actually having personal strength in your life is great, but admitting your weaknesses might even mean you're stronger. Whether you feel strong or weak, the point is that we love each other as we are and encourage each other with the strength of Christ.

As we sharpen each other, we become increasingly stronger. When iron metal is struck together, it refines the tool, strengthening it in preparation for building and edification. Similarly, we strengthen each other to build lasting and meaningful relationships. Rely on each other, but most importantly, rely on Jesus for your everlasting strength. When your friends are strong, continue to encourage them. When your friends are weak, show them that through vulnerability, Christ is able to shine his brightest light on us, give us power, and make us the beloved children of his kingdom.

Chapter 16
CIRCUS OF NUTCASES

In my second semester of college, I had a total of about three friends, and even that might be overstating it. At the beginning of the semester, I was introduced to two girls, Sydney and Lindsey. They look nothing alike, but for some reason, I would always mix up their names, and it took me forever to straighten them out. Sydney and Lindsey were childhood friends, and at the time, I didn't know that. Once I learned they were, it explained why they were so comfortable acting crazy around each other. When I was first introduced, I marveled at how comfortable they were with each other, and in an attempt to have that sort of confidence, I joined their silly stunts.

The first time I met Sydney and Lindsey, we were all studying in a building on campus. It was nighttime, so there weren't as many people as there were in the daytime. In fact, I think it was so late that it was only us in the building. We were studying long in to the night, and we were all getting a little bit antsy. For the first time, I was about to experience how deranged college students can become from their studies. After taking a few minutes of a break from grinding through our work, Sydney randomly proposed an idea. She said to get our stress out, we should all sprint around the building. Miraculously, we agreed to this.

With a quick burst, we were out the door running around like chickens with our heads cut off. We didn't just run, however. The maniacs in us also apparently wanted to scream. So there we were, alone on campus, sprinting around in circles and screaming like children. If someone had seen that, I'm certain we would've been booked into the nearest hospital immediately because something was terribly wrong. From that night, a friendship of wackiness brewed.

One of the next few times I spent time with Sydney and Lindsey, I headed over to their apartment after school one night. Sydney told me that they had planned to do some fitness activity in their apartment, and I was okay with joining them. I walked into their apartment, greeted by them with cheery faces and bright smiles. After a few minutes, I asked them to explain what kind of fitness routine we were doing.

"Oh, it's fitness dancing," Sydney informed me. "You watch the video and copy the guy dancing to the song."

I thought to myself, "You know, this is definitely not what I thought it was going to be, but I'm totally going to jam out."

We danced to a few songs, and I won't lie, they got me sweating. Plus, it was fun because we looked disastrous while trying to copy the dancers' complex and intense dance moves. The songs were good, but my favorite was one we danced to was by the one and only: Britney Spears. I bet you can guess which song we did by this chapter title. This wasn't just my favorite because her music has beats that make a crowd dance. It was my favorite because after the song, we decided that we were going to memorize the dance moves and do a performance. This was a cringe-worthy decision, but cringe-worthy decisions are the best decisions!

I kid you not, for almost three hours we tirelessly worked on perfecting every single move the dance-fitness instructor was doing. Finally, we had our finished product and were ready for a performance. The performance was even complete with an exercise ball, which we thought was a good addition since it looked like one of the giant balls found at a circus. The one flaw I now realize we had in our decision is that we decided to record it all. Yes, somewhere on Sydney's laptop exists a quite embarrassing recording of the three of us going all-in on a Britney Spears song, and I know that one day it will come back and haunt me.

In retrospect, I wouldn't have participated in a recording dancing to Britney Spears with just anyone, but Sydney and Lindsey radiated so much joy that it was hard to resist. They didn't care what other people would think when we ran around outside screaming. They certainly didn't care about the embarrassment of making a dance recording. Both of them were carefree because they wanted to have fun and be happy. Because of their enthusiasm, I was comfortable being myself. I wasn't scared to do things with them that other people might have been scared of doing because they may have been afraid of being judged.

I think that Jesus's Kingdom is a lot like this. His people put out so much joy that you can't help but join in the celebration. People run around screaming in delight, not caring if anyone looks upon them in puzzlement. They dance and they sing as much as possible, and they don't need to record anything because they're willing to do it time and time again. People decide to do instantly sprint around in freedom, shouting how great Jesus is because of the joy he's placed on their hearts.

There's not a lot of people who do spontaneous, unusual, or embarrassing things for fear of being ridiculed. Friends that will do these types of things with you are a rarity. We think that things could be a lot of fun if we did it, but we don't want to risk our egos and pride. Sitting back is comfortable for us because it ensures that we are safe from having our good reputation taken away from us. Nevertheless, if we don't take any risks, we never see a reward. We guard other people's perspectives of us so closely that it inhibits us from experiencing the fullness of life Jesus wants us to experience.

Psalm 16:11 puts it best: "You make known to me the path of life; in your presence there is fullness of joy; at your right hand are pleasures forevermore." With Jesus, the path of life is full of joyous moments. Experiencing these moments isn't possible if we don't rise from our seats and get to the entrance of the path that he's showing to us. The trail might not seem appealing to you, even though at the entrance there's a big, flashing, LED sign that says, "Extreme joy ahead!" It's not appealing because you don't want to take the risks of all the eyes watching you as you walk through the entrance. A word of advice: you can't see everyone staring if you don't look back.

The joy of Christ is contagious, and he calls us to spread this joy to others. He tells us to go to the entire world and make disciples. What is the good in keeping this joy all to ourselves? If his beaming light doesn't make you want to shine it on everyone you encounter, then have you really experienced it? Undoubtedly, it's daunting when Jesus unexpectedly calls us to run joyously down an unknown path. It's worrisome because we trust our own plans more than his, and are fearful of the potential outcomes. We worry about what will happen when we go out into the world to spread this joy, but I think deep down inside us we also know that there's potential for something truly supernatural to occur in the hearts of the world. How do we get to experience this kind of joy? It comes from three things: being connected to Jesus's presence in our lives, having faith in the future he has planned for us, and being a light to the people around us.

Knowing Jesus as a source of joy can be confusing, especially since he was the one who took all of our sin and shame upon himself and had sorrows because of it. But this joy is not a kind of joy where everything is all smiles and bubbliness. The joy that comes from Jesus is about victory and overcoming the grave. His joy doesn't exclude tears and heartbreak, rather it comes from realizing that he is good and everything he does will work together for our good. Being connected to his presence and remembering his promises is how we experience this true joy.

Being carefree stems from the fact that we trust that his promises will be fulfilled. When we have confidence that he will deliver, spreading his joy and taking a leap of faith onto the path ahead gives us assurance to keep going even when we feel the eyes watching us. Joy to this degree won't care about any discouraging eyes looking upon you, because if they watch you long enough, they'll probably catch a little joy, too.

Taking the risk to cover yourself in near-embarrassing joy will catapult you into rewarding relationships. You won't care about what others think because the joy of Christ inside you will be too much to contain, much like Sydney and Lindsey displayed. More importantly, you'll be able to show your friends that joy isn't just about putting on a happy face, but that it's about hope in Jesus's promises of liberation. Happiness and sadness exist in friendships, but it's the deep sense of joy that sharpens the connection between friends and adheres our hearts to Christ.

Joy is the substance that keeps relationships alive. Without joy, our friendships will start to deteriorate and lose meaning. How often do you want to visit a friend in an atmosphere that has no hope and feels mundane or meaningless? Jesus is all about bringing meaning into the meaningless, and to mirror his example, we must have expectations that every encounter with another person will have a profound impact on their perspective of love. If these encounters mean you have to act like a nutcase to plant seeds of joy in their soul, then I say absolutely join that circus.

Chapter 17
Two Strange Things

There are some things in this life that just shouldn't be tampered with. For example, some food should just not be messed with, namely salsa. I've already expressed my deep love for the nectar of heaven, but I think it's worth reiterating. Salsa is salsa and it should not be meddled with. You can add spice or other ingredients to add flavor, but you can't change the makeup of it and still call it salsa. Criminal charges should be pressed against anyone who attempts at disgracing the dignity of it. Why am I saying this? It's because I once witnessed a stranger putting a peculiar ingredient in my favorite snack.

Technically, he wasn't a stranger. I had met him once before, and this was my second time hanging out with him. His name is Clay, he's from east Texas, and I met him through one of my roommates. Clay had visited my roommate, had enjoyed our friend group, and had invited me to hang out with him in east Texas. At first, I wasn't so sure. I knew nothing about him, and I would have to drive hours away from home to arrive at his location. He seemed like a nice guy, though, so decided I decided to begin my journey to east Texas.

Upon arriving, Clay gave me a warm welcome and said our first order of business was to go to his favorite Tex-Mex restaurant in town. Obviously, I love Tex-Mex, so I happily obliged. Clay hyped this restaurant up, so my standards were set high, especially since Tex-Mex is my favorite type of food. When we arrived, it wasn't anything too crazy, just a regular restaurant with good smells drifting out from the kitchen. It was what would occur next that was crazy.

We sat down, and our waitress brought out some water followed by some chips and salsa. Then, Clay told me the tradition that east Texans do with their salsa. Apparently, it's an "east Texas thing" to squirt butter in your salsa. Yes, you read it right. A common custom was to squeeze a dollop of butter into heaven's nectar. I believed him, too, because as I looked around, I noticed there was a container of squeezable butter conveniently placed on each table.

I watched in disbelief as he grabbed the bottle and squeezed a stream of butter into the salsa. He was ruining it, he was going to clog my arteries, and I would be eternally scarred by what I saw. He stirred the mixture in anticipation while I watched on with disgust. I was mortified and scared by what I was about to put in my mouth.

"Alright, here you go, buddy," he said as he pushed the salsa bowl towards me.

With hesitation, I grinned out of courtesy and picked up a chip. I scooped it up, and crunched down into the unknown. Clay looked at me with curiosity, wondering if I would like his east Texas creation. I won't lie, it wasn't exactly bad, but I definitely prefer salsa as it's made to be. The butter gave it a unique taste, and I'd do it again, but only in east Texas.

For the duration of my stay, Clay took me in like we had been friends for years. He showed me around his town and told me all of his favorite things about it. He introduced me to his friends, gave me food, and a bed to sleep in. He was hospitable and kind; he even took me to the local mall and bought me socks as a welcome gift. We were driving around and laughing like it was the two hundredth time we hung out instead of the second.

There were two strange things I thought were strange about my visit to Clay. The first was that he put butter in salsa. Who does that? The second is that Clay took me in when I was a stranger. He gave me all the necessities and more, yet I hardly knew him at all. He showed me kindness and companionship even though we had no connection beforehand. If a random person showed up at my door and asked to come inside, my initial reaction would to be skeptical and say no, so Clay's hospitality was quite surprising. I could have been a criminal, and I could have stolen from him. Even so, Clay welcomed me with no restraint.

In the same way that Clay took me in when I was a stranger, Jesus does the same for us. He loved us and called us friend even when we didn't know him. When we haven't been connecting with him and have grown distant, he takes us back like nothing ever happened. He gives us everything we need and more and gives us shows us the way he does things, even though we may not like it.

A story Jesus tells that exemplifies this hospitality is the parable of the Good Samaritan. A man was traveling to Jericho, where he was beaten and robbed of his possessions, even his clothes. He was left lying on the ground left for dead. Two people, including a priest, passed by him and didn't give him a second glance. When the Samaritan passed by the man, he took him in, bandaged his injuries, and paid for the man to have a roof over his head.

Even though the Samaritan didn't know this man, he saw the importance of nurturing strangers. Jesus not only took us in when we were strangers, but sinners as well. Sin is what separates us from God, and while we were still sinners, he died for us. Therefore, before we confess our sin and accept his gift, we are the biggest strangers to God possible from our perspective. Jesus, however, knows us deeply, and we are anything but unfamiliar to him. Following Jesus's example, to show this spread this kind of love, we must be willing to invite even the most suspicious and dejected outsiders.

Jesus doesn't care about our past or what we've done. You could be in the best condition of your life, and that would be great to him. You could also be in the worst spot of your life, and he would accept you just the same. Instead of caring about our pasts, Jesus cares about our future with him. This is why he takes us in so willingly. He wants to ensure that his friend and child is taken care of, even when we make him a stranger to us in hope that we will cling to him the rest of our days. His desire for us to cling to him doesn't stem from selfishness; rather, it is a genuine extension of his aching heart for the lost and the outcast.

The first step in having a nurturing spirit towards everyone is to take care of our friends. If we can't love our friends in every aspect of their physical, mental, and spiritual health, then how can we expect to love complete strangers? Even if our friends shut the door on us and no longer want to pursue us, we must commit to having an open door policy. An open door policy means that all are welcome to come in, no matter where they've been traveling, what they look like, what they've done, or how they define their personality. It means that no matter what you're doing or what time of day it is, they are welcome to come in to your life for any reason.

Cultivating a spirit of hospitality isn't a matter of repetition. Opening the door to others won't sharpen any spirits if it's done out of obligation and an aggravated heart. Rather, hospitality comes from a craving to shelter every individual that needs it. If you're taking someone in, and they can tell by your outward expression that you're annoyed at them walking through the door, don't be surprised if they walk out of your life. Every stranger, friend, and everyone in between should be met with a nurturing, eager spirit.

Maybe you're thinking that you can't be that hospitable to strangers because you're shy or weird around people you don't know. Lacking a personality that allows you to easily become acquainted with people doesn't mean you are unable to have a welcoming spirit. Every person has unique ways in which to serve others. You know what you're good at, and you know the traits Jesus gifted you that allow you to contribute something that no one else can. Focusing on using these gifts to serve others is the perfect way to show care to others. 1 Peter 4:8-10 puts it this way: "Above all, love each other deeply, for love covers over a multitude of sins. Offer hospitality to one another without grumbling. Each of you should use whatever gift you have received to serve others, as faithful stewards of God's grace in its various forms."

What this all boils down to at the end of the day is loving your neighbor. We are called to love our neighbor as ourselves. I would even venture to say that we should show more love to our neighbor than to ourselves. This doesn't mean to completely ignore yourself - it means to put other's needs before your own. When you show love to other people, do so by loving them as if someone else was loving you. If you would want to be shown compassion when you're in a dark time in your life, then show them an abundance of compassion. If you would want someone to spend time with you when you're lonely, then spend an entire day with them. You get the picture.

Envisioning a world in which everyone is kind and hospitable to each other is a strange concept. Going through every door and entering every life being met with eager care seems weird. The only reason it seems weird is because the world isn't like that, and we have a hard time seeing ourselves be that way. The reality is, we are selfish human beings, and every decision we make we want to point back to us in some way. We want our hospitality to be praised and recognized so that it will make us feel good. When our selfish ambitions overcome our passion to attend to people, we have to take a step back and refocus our center of attention to Jesus. Making ourselves feel good isn't the mission; the mission is to serve others so they feel good and are drawn to the heart of Jesus.

Having a heart with an open-door policy means Jesus might ask you to do some things you aren't sure of. He probably won't ask you to put butter in your salsa, but he might ask you to step out of your comfort zone and befriend a total stranger. We might prefer to not engage with people we don't know, and we may be proven wrong about our preferences. Regardless, it isn't about what we prefer, it's about what Jesus wants to do. It might be uncomfortable, but Jesus doesn't operate in comfort zones. He operates with no boundaries, inviting every passerby, wanderer, and stranger into life with him.

As we grow more accustomed to being with our friends, we tend to lose something along the way. The original excitement of a new person and our responsiveness to satisfy their need to belong seems to be carried away with the winds of time. Our lost hospitality can lead to conflicts and friction in friendships. If you want to sharpen a friendship that has become dull, go find that excitement that blew away. Bring it back to you and be quick to provide your friends with everything they need and more. Before they even say a word, put what they need and more in their hands. Sacrifice yourself and your possessions for the sake of their well-being. Then the friendship will reignite, and you'll find that same enthusiasm for each other as you first did. In this way, we can learn to open the door to every stranger who passes by and love each other like Christ loves us.

Chapter 18
POOR KID

I've always admired people who can do impressions. Whether that's impressions of people or animals, it's neat that they can make themselves sound exactly like something else. My friend Alec can do the best goat/sheep impression I've ever heard. His bleat sounds exactly like a real goat. He's done it a few times, and people get confused because they think there's an actual goat in the room. Besides being impressive, his impression is really funny. Watching him bleat like a goat is hilarious because you wouldn't expect for that sound to come out of his mouth.

I never thought he would be able to practically use his skill in any situation, but when we went on our trip to Haiti, he put it to good use. The place we stayed at in Haiti was enclosed by high gates, and up on the hill, there were a few goats roaming around. The Haitians main purpose for these goats was to use them for milk and meat. Unsurprisingly, our American petting zoo enthusiasm wanted to get up close to the goats and touch them. Approaching them within petting range would be no easy task, as these goats were skittish and likely knew their eventual fate.

Alec and I ran up and down the hill, trying to touch at least one of them. We tried corralling them, luring them, and sprinting after them. Despite our efforts, we were no match for the goats; they were too evasive. As we let the goats run away, we saw some rustling in a bush close to us. Trotting around the brush was a goat kid. He was just a small lad, frolicking around playfully on the hill. Alec knew this was a perfect opportunity to make his wild petting zoo dreams come alive.

Harnessing the power of his inner goat, he began to bleat at the kid in attempt at some form of communication. I think his goal was to tell it to come towards us, but it must've heard something bizarre, because it stood there looking at us in confusion. This was progress, though, because we couldn't even get the other goats to stand still for more than two seconds. Slowly, Alec stepped toward the goat and paused. There was no reaction from the baby goat - it still stood there staring in bewilderment.

This was looking to be in our favor. Since Alec was the expert in goat communication, I stood back and watched him as he crept closer and bleated softly. It was a comical sight to behold, but I had to hold in my laughter to keep from scaring it away. Inch by inch, he walked toward the kid with cautiousness. It was like they were long lost brothers who were about to be reunited. Alec was born to be the goat whisperer.

Alec was now very near to the kid, and the air was intense as I knew what he was about to do. He wasn't right next to it, but he was close enough that if he ran, he would be able to touch it. If he took another step, it would probably run away, and we would leave empty-handed, having failed our goal. Alec waited a few seconds and then made his move. He sprinted like a cheetah to his prey and leapt toward the kid. In a flashy blur of Alec and baby goat, the score was officially settled. Alec came up victorious, chuckling as the kid sprinted across the hill back to the rest of its family.

Later that evening, we sat down around a large table awaiting a meal that some Haitian women had graciously prepared for us. While carrying on casual conversations, I noticed something that was out of the ordinary. There on the preparation table across the room, sat the head of the animal that supplied the meat for our meal. The head laying there was from the poor kid that Alec had touched. Now I know why all the rest of the goats were so afraid. They knew if a human touched them, they would probably be the next meal.

Needless to say, we didn't eat too much of the goat soup they made us. It just felt wrong having that poor baby goat taken all because we wanted to pet it. Of course, I don't actually believe it was chosen because we touched it, but it was ironic enough to suppress an appetite. At the end of the meal, Alec said, "Well, at least it gave us food on the table." Even though I still felt bad for the goat, he was right.

Accidents like this happen all the time to me. I'll meddle with something and accidentally mess it up. The outcome will be negative, not on purpose, but it still ends up disappointing. It seems as if everything I touch, destruction follows. Regarding the goat, Alec had some valuable wisdom to share. He knew that something good could come out of a bad situation. Even though something unfortunate happen, there was still provision that ensued because of it.

Our relationships can have unfortunate things happen to them because of our actions as well. We toy with them like they are expendable because we want to get something out of it. We meddle and mess with them, only to end up in negative circumstances. Maybe the opposite is true. Maybe we didn't mean to mess with our relationships on purpose, but conflicts arise anyhow. After we see the consequences of our actions, we get caught up in viewing the situation as terrible, and the trajectory of the friendship can become murky. It takes wisdom to know that goodness can come out of these hardships and that these hardships won't last forever. Looking back on the adversities, you can see how the situation brought good into your friendship by showing you that you can make it through tough clashes and learning how to best serve one another.

The wisdom we need to see the good in bad situations doesn't come from our own understanding. Anyone has the ability to see good in situations, but it takes Godly wisdom to be see the circumstance from pure, unselfish, and humble eyes. When we try to see good in bad situations on our own, we usually attribute the good back to ourselves. Rarely do we ever take a minute to think about how we can use unfortunate circumstances to provide for others. This kind of wisdom I'm referring to is written about in James 3:17. "But the wisdom that comes from heaven is first of all pure; then peace-loving, considerate, submissive, full of mercy and good fruit, impartial and sincere."

Think of a time when you've been in a conflict of some sort with your friend. Things were pretty tense, and you both did some things that messed up the kindness in your friendship. You were probably caught up in the heat and focused on how you were going to fire your next shot. You lacked the wisdom to look at the argument and find a way to bring good out of it. The heavenly wisdom is almost like a how-to guide for any situation in life. In this situation, you would need to stop, lay down your desire to be the winner of the argument, and take a wise, heavenly approach.

The first step would be to purify your heart. This means decontaminating yourself of wanting to be "the winner" of the argument. Next, is taking action to make peace. Then, make yourself consider the other person's situations and feelings. How is what you say going to affect what they feel? Submit and confess to your wrongdoings, show mercy, and be genuine in wanting to alleviate the battle. Having this heavenly wisdom to guide you not only helps in conflicts, but it also offers direction in any other question, decision, or predicament that arises as well.

By possessing heavenly wisdom, we are able to gain better insight on how Jesus has been good to us, how he will be good to us, and how we can be good to other people. We like to say, "God is good all the time. And all the time, God is good." As much as that comes out of our mouths, we don't live like we believe it. When something goes awry, we say, "I thought God was supposed to be good. Doesn't God want good things for my life?" What we really mean by this phrase is: "Why am I not getting what I want? Why are things not going exactly the way I want them to?" Having heavenly wisdom, we wouldn't be asking these questions. Instead, we would have faith knowing that no matter what happens, God will use it for his good, and we will praise him because of it.

Oftentimes we won't be able to have perfect heavenly wisdom. That's why we have friends to fill us in on the parts we're missing. Friends give us the rest of the wisdom we need to navigate the confusing, dark, and outwardly bad trials of life. The rest of the wisdom we lack is Jesus. Jesus is an exact description of the wisdom depicted in James 3:17. He knows us inside and out, and even if we don't understand his purpose for our lives during the tribulations we face, he knows exactly what he's doing. When you see a friend feeling like a failure or feeling like the ruined everything, offer them a little bit of heavenly wisdom. He's the light that pierces the darkness and lets us see the good where we think there's none.

Chapter 19
JUST CALL ME

If you want to meet the king of awkward, just give me a call, and I'll set you up with an appointment. Seriously, I have an issue. I'm terribly awkward and quiet around people I just meet. Most of it stems from insecurities. I want them to like me, so I'm choosy in what I say so as not to say something that could scare them away. The story is no different when I first met Lauren. We were riding with mutual friends in the back seat of a car, and our conversation was full of cringe-worthy moments. I actually remember internally screaming because I wanted to be out of that car so bad. Who ever knew she would become one of my closest friends?

Lauren is so humble that she could probably have about a billion different talents, and nobody would know about them. The first time I heard one of her secret talents, we were yet on another car ride. We were singing along to music and jamming out. Next on the playlist was "Lean on Me" by Bill Withers, a true jam that can be belted from the heart. When that song comes on, there's no holding back. Screaming the song off-pitch is tolerated.

We were singing our hearts out to the verses, and that's when Lauren let loose. She belted it out, sang beautiful harmonies, and stunned me with her angelic voice. Once the song ended, I told her how amazing her voice was. Of course, she denied it, but I was being serious. She had major talent, and she was doing as "Lean on Me" instructed and swallowing her pride, but in the wrong context. The world needed to know of this extraordinary talent, so I told her I was going to tell my roommate who leads worship to listen to her. She pleaded with me not to and was adamant about not singing in front of him, but I denied her the luxury to make that decision.

I ended up telling my roommate, and it wasn't long before Lauren was up on stage leading people in worship. She was using her talents for God's glory, and I was unbelievably proud of her. She was being humble; she didn't want to make a scene over the fact that she had such a great voice. Now, she's able to share her talent while leading people to the presence of Jesus and is still humble and grateful she has that opportunity.

The song "Lean on Me" is a great song about friendship. It talks a lot about bearing each other's burdens, being accessible, and having hope for the future. It asks us not to be prideful, but to be vulnerable with our souls and let someone else come in and comfort your distress. The idea of leaning on each other is a fundamental part of all friendships. Think about it: when you take a picture with your friend, do you usually awkwardly stand side-by-side with them? No, you probably put your arm around them. Putting your arm around them symbolizes your closeness to them. It says that with that person, you're willing to rely on them in times of trouble and completely open up so that they can help you.

Relying on someone else isn't a bad thing at all. It shows that you have the humility to realize you can't do everything on your own. In fact, Jesus's desire for us is that we lean on him for everything we need. He wants you to put your arm around him and say that you completely surrender to him. Once you admit that you won't be able to make it over that mountain by yourself, the walking gets easier because you have someone supporting your every step.

Why are we so stubborn and dismissive of the idea of people helping us? Deep down, we know that we can't do everything on our own, but we become prideful and try to be the hero because we don't want to our pride to be hurt. We protect our pride so carefully and shun vulnerability because we're afraid people will know the real us. We're afraid that if we let people in, we'll be seen as weak. We're afraid they'll ridicule us, expose our secrets, or not like what they see. It doesn't matter what you reveal to them, because what they see does not define you. Your identity comes from being a child of God.

Lauren was humble about her singing talents, and being humble is a characteristic essential to living a life full of Christ. However, it's possible to mix humbleness and vulnerability. Being transparent is what allows people to know you deeper. Lauren didn't boast about her talents, but instead she showed them to me in a way that didn't exalt herself. She showed me a part of her that rarely anyone else knew until she was recognized for her ability.

When friends are openly vulnerable, we are required to show them empathy. Empathy and service to one another is what gives us that warm feeling inside drawing us near to our friends. Empathy doesn't simply entail the understanding of one another's feelings, rather it is a deep connection involving the sharing of emotions. Even if you've never felt their specific emotion, empathy is striving to feel it regardless of any affliction it may cause. Friends need us to be empathetic when they're vulnerable, because if we aren't, we affirm all of their fears about opening up, even if those fears are irrational.

Although being empathetic to your friends is the biggest part of deepening your friendship through mutual vulnerability, you can't stop there. You need to cap it off with action. This is where accountability comes in to play. Without accountability, negative emotions are only temporarily altered, and positive emotions warp into pride. Both positive and negative emotions are healthy to an extent, but it's the balance of these emotions through action that keeps us grounded. Having someone to keep you in check confirms that these emotions are realized (whether positive or negative), we keep standing on solid ground, and life change occurs because of these feelings.

Ever since that awkward car ride, Lauren and I have become close friends. I can rely on Lauren to be there for me whenever I need it. Lauren is vulnerable, keeps me accountable, and is the most empathetic person I know. She truly cares for the feelings of others and does everything in her power to be a comforter. I know that if I needed Lauren at any time, I could just call her and she'd be there in an instant. She makes herself accessible so that if anyone needs her, she'll drop her schedule almost every time and make them a priority. When you look into Lauren's eyes when talking to her about anything, you can tell that she is sharing your emotions.

Even though Lauren is readily available as a reliable friend, the truth is she can't always be there, and neither can anyone else. What about in the dead of night when thoughts are crushing you and your friend's phone is on silent? What about in those moments where you can't bring yourself to reach out to anyone? There's only one who is always accessible no matter what where, or when, and his name is Jesus. He offers his shoulder to lean on when you're falling down. He's sitting by your bedside in the dark nights when you don't think you can make it another hour. He's there to listen whenever you need to talk.

Jesus not only is present when we need him, but he feels our deepest sorrows along with our greatest joys. He took the pain of the world upon him when he was put on the cross, so he knows more than anyone else combined what you're feeling. He understands the holes formed within us, and he comes to fill them up with his love. The only way you'll truly be fulfilled when you're longing for someone to be by your side is to turn to Jesus. He's the only one who's with you every minute of every day.

Completely leaning on each other doesn't always come in an instant. Sometimes, it takes a lot of time before you'll be comfortable with being vulnerable and honest about certain aspects of your life. It took a while before Lauren was able to display her talents to me because she wasn't comfortable with me at first. When friends become share sensitive emotions and put their heart in your hands, treat it with extreme care. Likely, this is information that they only trust a few people with and are confiding in you to safeguard their hearts with delicacy. Likewise, when our friends show us their skills and gifts, we should magnify this exponentially. We need to reinforce their gifts because it solidifies you as an important stronghold they can turn to when they stop believing their gifts have value.

The verse that gives us insight on how to be empathetic to our friends is Ephesians 4:2. "Be completely humble and gentle; be patient, bearing with one another in love." Patience is extremely important when taking part in your friends' emotions. If they're angry, you may feel that anger is directed toward you, but it isn't meant to be focused on you.

All they're doing is outwardly expressing their inner feelings. Being patient and peaceful during rants shows them that you are a steady anchor in their storm, just like Jesus is for us.

The awkwardness of initial friendships will eventually fade away. When you make a new friend, or you haven't spoken to someone in a while, the air can feel uncomfortable surrounding you. With time, the embarrassing edginess will disappear. When we haven't spoken with Jesus in a while, we can feel uneasy and unsure of what to say. We become insecure and ashamed of our lack of attempt for communion with him. Jesus acts a lot different than we do. He welcomes you back into his arms like you never left him. There's no awkwardness, only a joy that you have returned to be in his company.

Letting yourself be known doesn't have to be intimidating. It takes time to find solid shoulders to lean on, and once you do, you'll find a life that's full of meaning. We are to be the sharpeners of iron. If we make ourselves unavailable, they'll stay dull because they'll be trying to refine themselves against a sharpener that doesn't work. Be vulnerable, empathetic, and hold your friends accountable. You know that they have so much potential stored up in them, so help them realize that potential by keeping them on course. Point them to Jesus, because unlike you, his phone stays off mute during the night. Encourage them that they're just a word away from speaking to Jesus. When we call his name he answers us, and out of all of our friends, he's the sturdiest shoulder to lean against.

Chapter 20

THIS MEANS WAR

I won't lie, when my parents dropped my off for college and they left my new dorm room, I panicked. I was trying to hold myself together, but I felt alone. No one I knew was going there, I didn't have any friends yet, and I had no idea how to manage anything college-related. I was a helpless, scared little freshman who only knew how to use the microwave. Living completely on my own with virtually no support base within close distance was going to be a challenge that I didn't know I could take on.

Before our first day of classes, we had a dormitory meeting to go over all the basic rules and procedures. There, I learned that my Resident Assistant was Carolina, or Caro as she liked to be called. During my first encounter with Caro, she was quite the character. Her kind, loud, humorous, and exciting personality had the whole room on the edge of their seats. She told us that she would be like our hall's "mom", and we could come to her for help with anything. Whether it was a room issue, we had a bad day, or we just needed someone to hang out with, she said she was available.

Even though I appreciated her sympathetic words, I didn't take her up on this offer at first. After all, I didn't even really know what an RA was, and I figured that she'd be policing me most of the time. I decided to keep my distance, and I was still left friendless and timid. It was difficult the first few weeks living alone, and Caro had us all have one-on-one time with her so she could check in to see how we were doing. I went into her room, she gave me hot chocolate, and I told her about how different it was since I moved in. It was a nice conversation, but I didn't think much of it because I thought she was obligated to spend that time with me.

One day, I was walking back from class back to my dorm. Upon arriving at my door, I noticed something out of the ordinary and should definitely not have been visible to the public eye. On the bulletin board attached to my door was an embarrassing old photo of me and a clever caption. It was at this moment that I realized her true intention was to be friends with me. I also realized that she was out for blood. She had come for me, and I had not sent for her. Oh yeah, this means war.

I wasn't going to let her win this game, so I went through her social media profile and found a picture that would surely mortify her. I came up with the most savage caption I could think of, and I clicked 'print' with sassiness guiding my every move. I marched down the hall to her door and pinned the picture to her bulletin board, smug with satisfaction. A day later, I found yet another photo on my door. She was getting quicker and wittier, but I would not let her outdo me. The war continued, and soon we were close friends. We exercised, went to get tea, watched late night movies, and joked around together. She was my first friend in my new home.

Since we became friends, my entire demeanor changed. At first, I was nervous and frightened about everything. I would shy away from people and events because I was afraid of being alone in new situations. Caro inspired me to have strength and courage, and she did this by choosing to invest her time in me. She showed me that I was not alone, and that I had the potential to flourish there. She emboldened me with her words, unashamed demeanor, and confidence in me.

If you're anything like me, you underestimate what you can do in new situations. We have no reason to doubt ourselves, but unfamiliar environments suppress our confidence. Not only do we underestimate ourselves, but we tremendously underestimate Jesus's power. For the record, his power is not to be misjudged. You were made in his image, and he wouldn't have sent you into the war he did if he didn't believe you could do it. Jesus will never hand you a situation that you can't brave.

We lose confidence in unfamiliar situations because we've grown accustomed to living a safe life. We live in our protected, routine environments that cushion us from progressing in our undeveloped potential. We're scared to tap into that potential because we won't know how to manage it or that no one will be around to support us. Take a look at yourself in the mirror. What you see, Jesus created the precise way he intended it to be. Every hair on your head, every shade of color in your eyes, and even everything you perceive to be a flaw. The characteristics you love about yourself and the traits you don't like were crafted into you for a purpose. Jesus sees you as his seamless creation, and one of his greatest joys is seeing us reach our highest capability.

Think of what you're most capable of, and then erase that thought and think bigger. With Jesus, there's no limit to his capability. With him, all things are possible – even the impossible. He has a knack for doing big things – life-changing things. Everything you doubt about yourself he can obliterate in the blink of an eye. Deuteronomy 31:6 instructs us, "Be strong and courageous. Do not be afraid or terrified because of them, for the Lord your God goes with you; he will never leave you nor forsake you." There's something so blatantly obvious but so strangely difficult for us to comprehend in this verse: you are not alone!

When I first arrived at my dorm, I allowed fear to overtake me, and it inhibited me from seeing that when I was dropped off, I was never alone. Jesus was always there to be my comfort. Fear can do things like that. Fear can blur our vision and cause us to see things that aren't there and prevent us from seeing things that are there. When our fears start to corner us, we have to make the decision to either run far away or to stand our ground. Personally, I'd like to choose the latter. Jesus is an immovable defense to everything that

THIS MEANS WAR

attempts to bring destruction upon us, and invincibility sounds like a fantastic option against impossible odds.

Fear is one of satan's best tactics in luring our concentration away from Jesus. He can use it to infiltrate even the tiniest crack in your defenses. He knows that when we succumb to fear, we start to identify with them more than we identify ourselves with Christ. He tells us that we're not strong enough, not brave enough, and not fill-in-the-blank enough to achieve Jesus's plan for our lives. When you hear these whispers in your ear, you can tell the enemy that you've got something that will make him more fearful than he could ever make you. And trust me, he will pee his pants when you tell him this: Jesus has already won the war.

You read that right, the battle has already been decided. Jesus became victorious when he defeated death and rose out of the grave to tell the enemy and sin that it had no power over him. But he didn't claim the victory for himself; he claimed it for the world. You and I get to share this triumph over the darkness. Everything the enemy tries to do to lure you to his side is in vain. Once you accept your victory in Christ, there is absolutely nothing he can do to ever tear you from Jesus's grip. Frankly, I don't even know why the enemy is still trying. He might be trying to get a stronghold, but he already knows what's going to happen. His day is coming, and Jesus is going to make all of the enemy's strongholds look beyond pitiful compared to his glory.

When I entered the embarrassing picture war with Caro, it was all in good fun. What she was really doing was leading me into another war – a war against the lies that were trying to drag me down. The lies were telling me I was alone, had no chance of succeeding, and I didn't have what it took to achieve my dreams. Caro knew otherwise, and she saw the need to step in and give me the boost of confidence to strike down those lies. Jesus does the same thing for us. He leads us valiantly into battle because he knows the enemy stands no chance. He equips us with the strength and courage to fight off the deception attacking us.

For some of us, it's easy to find the resilience and bravery to go into battle. For others, it's a challenge. Some may already be wounded by the enemy, left to wither away. They're bleeding out from the cuts the enemy made and don't have the power to fight on their own. This is where we get to come rushing in to fight the battle with them. Battles aren't meant to be fought on their own, but alongside others who are united for the same purpose. The ones who aren't wounded get to run in with our iron, sharpen their tools to fight, and defend the injured against the schemes of the enemy.

Jesus is the hero of our battles, running in to protect us while he also heals us from our wounds. He inspires us to get up and keep fighting alongside our brothers and sisters. Without him, we wouldn't have the strength or the courage to face the barrage of assaults the enemy launches our way. The most important thing we need to remember is that we're not alone. When we feel entrapped and overwhelmed on all sides as the darkness closes in, Jesus is behind us, ready to shine his beaming light to drive away the darkness.

To inspire our friends to not give in to lies and deception, our duty is to embolden and protect them. If you possess the bravery to stand up and fight for yourself, then look beside you to your friend who has lost hope. Stand in front of them and show them you'll fight for them. Tell them they're worthy, loved, and capable of greatness. Show them that you fight for them not out of obligation, but out of deep love and service to lay down your life for their sake. Give them the boldness to stand up with fearlessness, knowing the battle has already been won.

Chapter 21
ALL ARE WELCOME

You can choose whatever friends you want to have, but you can't choose your family. Family is the group of friends you've been given to stick with you for the rest of your life. None of us get a book full of names and pictures to select from. There's no formula to tell us which parents or siblings we want. We are born into our family, and if you're fortunate enough to, those are the people you get for the remainder of your life.

I'll be honest, my family is a bunch of loons, and I love it. My dad is the handyman; he can fix anything and everything you bring to him. He probably gets annoyed that everyone always asks him for help, but when you're so good at it, what else do you expect? My mom is a teacher who cares for her students about as much as she cares for her family. However, don't be fooled - she isn't tame. Underneath that quiet persona is a wild woman waiting to be released. Sometimes we think that she's lost her marbles, but if she had all her marbles, she wouldn't be as fun. I'll admit, I definitely inherited my crazy from my mom.

My younger brother Micah is quiet but adventurous. He likes the outdoors, and especially likes the wildlife in it. His passion to care for animals reflects his desire to nurture all forms of life. My youngest brother Blake is strong and athletic. Even though he'll always be my little brother, he's undeniably passed me up in size. He has a tough shell, but we all know that underneath his shell is a mushy, lovable guy.

My family is unique and diverse, just as many families are. We've shared years of memories, laughter, and fun times. Nevertheless, my family has also had its share of fights, squabbles, and tough times. What's important about family isn't the amount of good times or bad times you have. None of those experiences should change how a family operates. A family operates under the notion that each member will be a pillar of trust and sustenance despite any member's shortcomings or downfalls. Trusting each other and giving support can be hard, especially when one of your family members does something that hurts you deeply or causes you anger. Forgiveness is essential to building trust in families. The people in your family are the people you've known the longest and should be the people who you can confide in.

Much like our own family, we have another family, and that family is comprised of our brothers and sisters in Christ. Each member is unique and offers something different that they can contribute. The family works together as one unit, with each person helping the other function. As brothers and sisters, we can trust each other to love even when love isn't the most appealing option.

I know that many times, love is not an appealing option for me even though it always should be. Sometimes, I would much rather explode in anger, ignore someone, or be vengeful. Even though love is not always the most appealing option, it is the most rewarding. That's why love is my favorite option. You don't always see the immediate results of love, and you might never get to. In today's culture, we live for instantaneous results. Everything we need is at the tip of our fingers through the use of technology, but people aren't technology. People aren't robots that don't need attention. People need time and love in order to thrive. We invest a lot of our time in technology because it gives us instant results and gratification. After those few seconds of gratification, it's back to wanting more. During all that time invested for a short burst of results, we could have invested it in someone else who will give us far more gratification than we could ever get from a screen.

Growing up, one way my family invested time in each other was eating together at the table every night for dinner. Believe me, there were times where I really did not want to be at that table. I would be annoyed with someone, I had a bad day, or I just didn't feel like talking. Eating together at dinner disregarded everyone's feelings about being at the table, and frankly, it didn't matter how I felt about being at the table. What mattered is that at the end of the day, everyone was at the table regardless of the circumstances. It was a statement that no matter what any of us were going through, we would all be there for each other.

Being brothers and sisters in Christ, we must also recognize that this family isn't exclusive. Seats at the table aren't only reserved for only Christ followers. All are welcome to the table. If we were an exclusive family, others would view the family as a clique and be discouraged from joining us at the table. Whether other people join us at the table is their choice, but it is our responsibility to invite them to have a seat with us. Jesus did not exclude anyone from being with him, nor did he have a certain criteria that had to be met. He sought out the ones who usually weren't invited to have a seat at the table, and those people got the best seats.

Relinquishing control is the key to trusting someone else. So often, we hold our lives, secrets, ambitions, and emotions tightly in our grip because we want to be the only one in control. We think we're the ones behind the wheel, when in reality, our car is being remote-controlled. Giving up control is giving up ownership. No one can have your trust if you're the sole owner of your life, secrets, ambitions, and emotions. Trust is dual ownership, if not multi-ownership. By having another owner, if something breaks in your life, someone else still has a part of you that's whole, and vice versa. Trust is not an agreement by the other party to keep things clean and shiny. When you trust someone, you need to understand that everyone is susceptible to mistakes. Trust is placing your confidence in someone that they will safeguard your life but knowing that there is room for error.

You're probably wondering why you should trust someone if you know they might make a mistake. The first reason is that trust catalyzes relationships, and without it, relationships stay stagnant. The second reason is that a mistake has the ability to reshape you. Whether it's your own mistake, or their mistake in breaking your trust, you get to learn from the situation and redefine a new version of yourself. The risk you take in trusting someone is not the possibility of being betrayed, but is the prospect of not showing forgiveness if it happens. Trusting in someone empowers them to form a stronger bond with you because you believe in their ability to have your back and be a devoted friend.

What I've found in following Jesus is that when you put your trust in him, things are far from clean and shiny, but he makes no mistakes. That's because he calls us to get our hands dirty and do the work that everyone else is afraid to do. If we sat back and just spoke what we believe, what good would that do? In order for us to have the best chance and gaining trust in people's lives, they need to see that we instinctively dig our hands deep into the dirt. When people see that you're willing to go into the mud to help them, they'll be a lot more willing to grab your hand and let you pull them out.

My family hasn't always gotten along with each other. There have been significant mistakes by all of us, but by Jesus's grace, there has been forgiveness. What I've seen by being in my family is that Jesus can be trusted to be many things. He can be trusted to be a handyman, relatable, nurturing, and lovable. When you put your trust in him, he never breaks that trust. Whatever you need to trust Jesus with, he can handle it. There's nothing you could ever bring to the table that he's not capable of being trusted with.

We're all really prone to making mistakes, but we need to try our best to not make mistakes with our friends' trust. Following the example of Jesus, we need to treat their confidence in us with the utmost respect. Trust is a rare commodity, and friends expect us to not break it. It may be a lot to handle, but friendships aren't meant to be an easy win. They take time to develop and adherence to each other's needs.

When people outside of the table see the deep trust between the people at the table, they will automatically be drawn in. When you recognize that someone is being drawn in, don't let the opportunity to invite them in slip away. If someone wants a seat at the table, they get one. It doesn't matter if they're not like us, what their political views are, where they came from, or any other factor. In the family of Christ, all are welcome.

Chapter 22
GRAM CAMP

Some people dream of going somewhere exotic for vacation. The blaring sun, white sand beaches, clear water, and island palm trees are some of the many features people desire for their ideal getaway. A tropical island sounds like a sweet escape or a glimpse of heaven away from the realities back home. Maybe the beach doesn't interest you, but instead you'd rather go on an expedition to the Amazon rainforest. It doesn't matter what glamorous vacation you choose, I'm telling you that you're dreaming of the wrong one. You need to enroll in a Gram Camp.

One summer, my friend Josh invited me and a few other friends to embark on a journey to his grandmother's house. He calls his grandmother 'Gram', hence the name Gram Camp. He advertised it as the week of a lifetime, filled with continuous hours of fun. Gram was kind enough to be willing to let a bunch of teenagers raid her house. Having no reason to turn down such a grandiose offer, I accepted, and we began the drive to Gram's house.

There was no false advertising, as everything Josh had promised was delivered. We played many board games, went on hikes, kayaked, and found a rope swing on the river that we used for hours. There were hours of laughter, and at the end of each day we were exhausted from all the fun we were having. Gram Camp was like a sweet escape from all the stresses at home.

Although Gram's hospitality, kindness, and the joy of Gram Camp were impressive, what stunned me the most was the game of pool. We played many hours of pool, but little did we know that a pool legend was among us. The legend wasn't any of the newcomers, but it was Gram herself. I have yet to do research, but I would be willing to bet she has had some type of career in pool in her history.

Luckily, we played in teams, and Gram was on my team. She was carrying us through the game; I was playing horribly. There was moment when, I kid you not, she took her shot from behind her back and sunk not one – but two balls! Unsurprisingly, we won the game, and I basked in the sweet victory of playing alongside a legend.

This may not seem like the ideal vacation to you, but it was to me. It's not the place that allows you to have fun – it's the people. Going somewhere with close friends and having a good time is my idea of a great vacation. It allowed me to escape and forget all the worries that were surrounding me at home. If it weren't for Josh and Gram, I never would have found this escape. They cultivated an environment in which we were able to let go and find peace in being in one another's presence.

Even if you're going through a good season of life, it's always good to have an escape every once in a while. When friends approach you, they obviously aren't looking to acquire more problems. They're looking to get away and clear their mind. They're looking for something that will bring joy to their hearts. Most likely, they're not even looking for a thing, event, or place that will make them happy. They're looking to spend quality time in your presence. That's what will truly allow them to escape and let go.

If you're looking for an escape, you can find it in Jesus. He offers an escape from everything that weighs you down and causes you to drag. You can find him in the buzzing of everyday life, but you can really find him in the silence and stillness of solitude. From all the garbage you're carrying, he offers a way out. After all, he did conquer death itself.

When your friends come to spend time with you, your demeanor should be that of a tour guide leading them on the most exotic vacation they've ever been on. Show them what beauties and treasures life holds. No one likes an apathetic tour guide. Be excited about their opportunity to escape with you! It's your time to put all the worries to rest and find a burst of energy!

During our kayaking at Gram Camp, we spotted that rope swing along the river and didn't think twice about using it. Nothing else mattered along the river except for that rope swing, and it took up all of our attention. We went through hours of climbing up and swinging back down. Every single swing was just as fun as the last one.

Friends come to other friends for an escape so that they can be refreshed, renewed, and focused on. If our attention is focused on other things while our friends are trying to capture our genuine attention, it sends a message that they are not as important to as they think. I can't think of a more disheartening message to send to a friend. They come to us, wanting nothing but to spend time fully immersed without distractions in each other's company, and instead we choose to pursue other things that bring us personal satisfaction. By committing to all the events in our lives that make us "busy" rather than blocking out time for our friends, we brand ourselves as unavailable and subconsciously show that our ambitions are more important than our friends' lives.

Don't get me wrong, there are necessities that we have to commit to in order to survive, but I'd be willing to bet there are a lot of things on your calendar you can easily mark off. I don't know how anyone else feels, but if a friend comes to me wanting to take up my time, they can have it. At the end of my life, I want to be able to look back and say that I committed to people exponentially more than I focused on material things.

Escapes give people the chance to lower barriers they would otherwise have up. If you give people your undivided attention, you may learn things you never would have known before. During that pool game at Gram Camp, if I would have been focusing on something else like my phone, I would have never seen her make that legendary shot. My mind would not have been blown, and I would not have known she was so good at pool.

Life is so much sweeter when you enjoy the moments in front of you. There are a lot of interesting things that capture our attention, but have you ever paused and been thankful for everything around you? Have you stopped to notice where you are and how great it is that you get to keep breathing air? Focus your attention on the people surrounding you because you never know how long you'll get to keep them.

What I learned from Josh and Gram is that friends offer an escape from whatever situation in life you're in. Josh invited me to a place he described as wondrous, and the promise was delivered. Gram was unbelievably kind enough to allow us to enter her home and be the source of this retreat. It's the people you're with that make moments memorable, not the places you go.

Similarly, Jesus offers us an escape. He offers to take us away from the weight of the world and be with him in his kingdom without any worry. He promises us a future without any pain or suffering, and he is faithful in fulfilling his promises. When he offers us this retreat, we get to escape death, sin, and the chains that bind us to the depravity we want to break free of. Jesus is excited to take you to this place he promises. More than that, he's excited to be with you because he cares way more about you than any place he could ever take you.

The tough thing about finding an escape is that we consider ourselves too busy to even make the time for one. The reality is, we flood our schedule with so many activities because we want to feel important. We want to feel like we are making an impact through keeping our calendars full. I would venture to say that you'll feel pretty good if you use a good portion of your time pouring into others instead of pouring into yourself.

Jesus being our escape doesn't mean that all of our troubles will suddenly leave us. Escaping means that we get to break free of the control our troubles have over our lives. Instead of being confined, we are free from our imprisonment. When Jesus left the tomb, he declared that death has no power over us. Our sin is no longer entitled to us, and it has no claim on our lives. Instead, we get to live our lives experiencing glimpses of heaven on Earth.

In order to sharpen our friends, we have to provide them an environment to be sharpened in. We have to commit our attention to them when they need it. We can't just blindly swing in the dark and hope we create sparks. Be excited about spending time with them. Carve out time that's devoted specifically for them. Don't miss a moment because you were distracted by something else. Be appreciative of the present and allow Jesus to work through your quiet thankfulness. Give them an escape to flee to so that you can experience abundant life and love them to the fullest.

Chapter 23

LOUD AND PROUD

In small town Texas, nothing gets more attention than a high school football game. Every Friday night is almost like a family reunion. People that you haven't seen in years all congregate around a patch of grass to watch teenagers run into each other. What a magical thing to behold. Of course, I was always too small to ever even think about playing football. Plus, I don't take too kindly to running when I don't want to, so the band was way more up my alley.

During the games, the band was almost like a second cheerleading unit. We had chants and cheers, but to be honest, they were more for us to have fun rather to cheer on the football team. We had one chant where we yelled at someone and said, "Hey (someone's name), how do you feel?" They would respond with, "I feel good, oh I feel so good!" It was simple, but a good way to get people involved in being rowdy if the mood was down.

Occasionally, we would ask the cheerleaders how they felt and they would respond as a group. However, I don't think they would have ever heard us if it weren't for Mikayla. Mikayla has been my friend since the 5th grade, and she is a loud 'n proud gal. Her voice and enthusiasm made her the perfect cheerleader, and she has a knack for honing in on any voice. It's almost like she was waiting for the moment I would yell over at the cheerleaders. She would immediately recognize it and respond in a moment's notice.

What most people recognize about Mikayla is how loud of a talker she is, but what they don't realize is how good of a listener she is. Sure, she can captivate a room, and I love that! She can also hone in to what you're saying and take it to heart. Just like when I yelled to the cheerleaders, she could hone in on my voice even when her surroundings were noisy and make sure that I was recognized. She's able to listen intently and respond accordingly.

There's a tremendous difference between hearing and listening. Hearing is your ear taking in sounds and sending signals to your brain. There's no purposeful effort behind it; it just happens. Listening is making the conscious decision to derive meaning from words and concentrate on what is being said. Mikayla heard the sound of my voice, but she chose to listen to what I was saying so that she could respond appropriately.

We're really bad at being listeners. In most conversations, we hear sounds coming out of the other person's mouth but don't actually listen to what they're saying. We hear a word that triggers something that we want to say, so instead of listening to the other person, we're thinking about the next thing we're going to say. Listening requires that we clear our minds of what we want to say and fill our minds with the words the other person is saying. Listening is not a matter of hearing another person's words, but critically thinking about them and then responding in a way that points the focus of conversation to them.

The hard thing about listening is that is usually requires silence and deliberate focus on our part. It's easy to jump in and interrupt someone so that you can give input and advice to them, and the motive is usually to help them. In order to pour into people as much as we can, they need to be as empty as they can, which means we need to let them say everything they want to say. There's major relief when everything that's bottled up gets released, and after all the bad stuff is emptied, we get to refill them with truth.

When we quickly interrupt someone with our own opinions or speech, it deters them from wanting to share with us. They will not want to speak out of fear that they won't get to say everything they need to say. They need the conversation to be on their immediate needs while we are selfishly focused on steering the conversation toward ourselves. Focus on the words they're saying, not the words you want to say in response. Your response will naturally come after you think about everything they have said to you.

Maybe this is why a lot of people are scared to talk to Jesus. They're afraid that he'll suddenly interrupt them with judgment and tell them what they're doing is wrong. They're afraid that their words will simply be words, only heard and not listened to. Jesus doesn't want to interrupt, nor does he want to condemn. He wants to listen intently because he cares. He cares about his children and wants to make sure that all of their emotions are validated. He'll listen for as long as needed and then fill you up with the truth you need to hear.

Our brains are hardwired to be social and think of quick responses, but remember that listening is a choice. Listening doesn't happen automatically. You have to train yourself to say, "I'm not going to think about what I want to say. I'm simply going to focus on what they're saying." You might even find you have a better response if you listen with the intent of not responding.

Mikayla has a lot of words to say, many of which come from her gifted wisdom. She also knows when to close her mouth, a skill that not many of us possess. Friends may not even want a response from you when they begin outpouring themselves. They may simply want you to listen without saying a word. They may want you to close your mouth, focus on the words they're saying, and acknowledge that what they said has meaning and is valid. Sometimes the best response is no response at all.

James 1:19 speaks of this, "My dear brothers and sisters, take note of this: Everyone should be quick to listen, slow to speak and slow to become angry." This was written with the goal to encourage real conversations as opposed to fake conversations that don't edify. This verse is also telling us to listen so that we don't jump to conclusions. When we listen to information, our first instinct is to react to it, and way may draw uninformed conclusions. After we listen to the remainder of the information, our whole perspective can change because we learned new information.

Especially when friends are telling us something important, the last thing they need is for us to jab in with our opinion and not let them finish. That can immediately close the door that they were trying to walk through with you. Listening goes against all of our instincts. Our instincts say, "Be quick to speak and slow to listen," but we have to retrain ourselves to do the opposite.

A way we can sharpen our friends is leading through listening. I could tell that Mikayla was a great leader for her fellow cheerleaders not solely because of her skills, but by her ability to attend to each individual person. Leadership doesn't mean that you have an outspoken personality, are aggressive, or possess more skills than someone else. A big part of leadership is that you take into account everyone else's words and become a servant. The best leaders are often humble, soft-spoken, and aren't the first one's you would peg to be the front-runner.

Jesus was by no means a front-runner when he walked the Earth. He was born in a very humble setting and often retreated so he could be alone. He doesn't even want to be the front-runner; he wants you to be. That's why he listens so intently to any of our problems, celebrations, downfalls, and accomplishments. He wants a meaningful relationship, and part of the way that relationship flourishes is by deriving meaning from the words you speak to him.

If we are quick to speak, that doesn't sharpen our friends. It prevents them from being sharpened, and if anything, it dulls them. Listen without an intent to respond. Place value on your friends' words and affirm that what they say has meaning. Even if it seems small, do everything in your power to bring meaning into it. That's what Jesus is all about – bringing meaning into seemingly meaningless things.

Just like Mikayla seemed like she was on the alert for my voice, Jesus is on the alert as well. He's waiting for you to talk to him and tell him everything that's going on. He wants to hear all the joys and hardships of your life. He already knows them, but it means so much more when he gets to focus on the words coming from the mouth of his child. Let's be like Jesus in the way that he is eager to hear what we have to say, and let's respond to our friends out of a selfless desire to see our friends sharpened. In this way, we show our friends that our love for them is loud and proud.

Chapter 24

PASTA SHIRTS

Do you remember the first time you met one of your friends? Do you remember what that moment was like to know you would make countless memories with them? Sometimes a single moment can set the tone for a friendship that will last a lifetime. One joyful encounter sets off a chain reaction for a lifetime of companionship and a bond that can endure the most violent storms. You didn't expect for the friendship to turn out the way it did, but here you are. Hopefully, you have someone like this in your life such as a childhood friend.

The name of the friend I have like this is Reagan. She's also known as "Day Full of Rea" because she gushes rays of joy in your day just like sunshine. Reagan and I have gone to school together through high school but started our friendship in middle school. Reagan is the type of person who has a humor that involves craziness and oftentimes random acts of senseless hodgepodge. Any ordinary person might shy away from this humor, but it's exactly my kind of funny. Reagan and I have a unique friendship that has played a vital role in my life. We've traveled the world, laughed, cried, gone through tough times, and gone through times of jubilant abundance. Though we have been through many times together, I wouldn't change one thing. She never judges you, and she will always have your back you no matter what. She gives advice that is for the benefit of my life and has always been a steady support beam through sunshine and rain.

I named this chapter "Pasta Shirts", but I could have named it anything. I could have named it "Take Our Picture" for the times we were being obviously rambunctious just so we could have a camera pointed at us. I could've named it "B Team" for when we went from being on literally the worst Ultimate Frisbee team in the state to winning the state championship the next year. I could've named it "Drive In" for all the times we would sit at a fast food drive in and talk about life. I could've named it "Deer in the Headlights" for when I accidentally walked up on her using the restroom in a bush while backpacking, and she froze in terror. I could've named it "Wild, Wild Motochildren" for the time we rode motorcycles in Haiti (which I will tell in this chapter). However, even with the plethora of memories I could have picked from, I chose to name it "Pasta Shirts" because that was the moment that set the tone of our friendship that will last a lifetime.

When I was in middle school, I barely knew Reagan. Not only did we go to the same school together, but we attended the same church as well. During my first church camp was when I first experienced Reagan's undomesticated personality. We were playing messy games outside, and one of the games was a pasta war. The only object of the game was to get each other as messy as possible. These particular noodles were disgusting. It was blazing hot outside, so you could see the vapor in the bag of the noodles. When you put your hand in the bag to grab a handful, they were saturated with a warm, repulsive slime. During this fight, I had not even thrown one noodle at Reagan. I'm an advocate for a fair fight, but she had other plans. Without warning, I felt my shirt being pulled from the back and the disgusting mass of pasta slide all the way down my back. I whipped around to see the culprit to find Reagan hysterically laughing at me. There's a picture of her committing this heinous crime against me, but don't be fooled – I got her back.

That was the first time I experienced Reagan's bursts of playfulness, but if you think she's wild from that story, think again. Trust me, she is not that tame. She was already wild as a middle schooler, but her enthusiasm for craziness exponentially increased over time. Although that story is a good representation of her carefree demeanor, I want to tell another story that encapsulates her joy. When we were freshman in high school, our youth pastor took me and Reagan, along with a few others, on a mission trip to Ferrier, Haiti. We were getting ready to travel to another village to help install water pump filters, and our method of travel was motorcycle.

Before this, we had never ridden on a motorcycle before, and we looked incredibly clueless when trying to get on. It took us an absurd amount of time to get situated, but we finally managed to climb aboard. There we were, smiling with a cheeky grin and cheesy visors, ready to ride with our Haitian friend who had been laughing at us trying to get on the motorcycle. Once we were all ready, we took off toward the village. If anyone were to see us riding that motorcycle, they would probably describe it as two rabid, baby lemurs thrashing in excitement. Reagan was shrieking in laughter the entire ride, which was in turn causing me to scream. Our driver was probably so annoyed with us, but we were so engulfed in the thrill. Once we got on a long road scattered with gravel, our motorcycle increased speed. Our parents didn't need to know this, but I would be willing to bet that we exceeded speeds of ninety miles per hour.

When our motorcycle increased speed, Reagan squeezed me to hold on and proceeded to jab her fingers into my side to try and make me jump. She also put her mouth right up to my ear and was wheeze-laughing very audibly. This monkey was trying to make me die! Of course, I thought that was hysterical and couldn't breathe as tears from my laughter welled up in my eyes. With the wind whipping through our hair, we rode the whole way to the village with loud laughter while she was basically trying to kill me. When we arrived at the village, our driver let us off and looked at us and couldn't help but laugh at our appearance. What a wild, wild ride.

As I mentioned earlier, there are countless other stories I could write about Reagan. However, one of the most notable things about her is that she's wild. She has an untamed spirit that ventures wherever the wind takes it. There's no fear in her: she hops up on that motorcycle, throws on a crazy face, and is ready to ride. I think she's so wild, in fact, that she has the ability to love people for who they are. She's not afraid to show people who she truly is, and that lets her love the crazy in other people. Like Reagan, I share this crazy spirit. Few people ever get to see this side of me, but because of her unconditional love, I'm completely unrestricted.

Many times, crazy friendships begin with a single moment that sets the precedent for the rest of your life. Reagan was fearless and unbroken in the way that she sprinted full speed and toothy grin to squish a handful of that slimy pasta down my shirt. To her benefit, this tendency to sprint full speed translates well into everything she does in life. She pursues her dreams with a fiery passion and invests heavily into helping other people pursue their dreams. That single moment of slimy, disgusting peril catapulted me into believing what Reagan was offering. It helped me realize what friendship is, helped me to believe in myself, and allowed me to trust her even when she was trying to make me unstable on a motorcycle on a gravel Haitian road.

Being a follower of Jesus means that you're in for a wild ride. You're also in for some wild love. Do you remember the first moment you truly encountered his love? It might have been surprising and unexpected. You didn't anticipate someone running toward you to suddenly bring you so much joy into your life. Or maybe you haven't encountered his love, but chances are that if you turn around, he's right behind you about to smother you in a lot of it. This first encounter with him will throw you in to a never-ending story of memory after memory. You'll have so many different chapters of your life, each about a special moment you shared with him.

Being a friend of Jesus is a lot like that motorcycle ride in Haiti. Sometimes in your life, you'll reach high speeds. Everything will seem like it's flying around you, and you're left grasping for something to hold on to. Sometimes you'll be on a gravel road. The path will seem bumpy or unclear, and you'll struggle to gain traction while the bumps are tossing you around. Sometimes you may not even know how to get on the motorcycle in the first place. You've never gone through this situation before, and you're not sure what to expect or how to handle it.

Despite all uncertainty, Jesus is the answer to all fears. He is fearless as a roaring lion. His love is wild and untamed. His Word tells us that his love is so powerful, that nothing could ever separate us from it. Not death, any power, any creature – nada. He'll join you on the wild ride of life, smiling from ear to ear as he loves you for who you are. He believes in you, and he wants to help you pursue your wildest dreams. In your darkest hour, he gushes rays of sunshine that will light you up if you only open the blinds.

As much as you think you don't need it, we all need a little crazy in our lives. We need wild, untamed, fierce, and joyful love to cover us every day. We need friends who won't judge us but will love us in every detail of our being. When you're with your closest friends, you should be able to hide nothing from them. Every aspect, no matter how absurd, of your personality should be brought to exuberant life.

When you're wild with your friends, think back to that one moment that sparked the friendship in the first place. Think of all the memories that spawned from that first encounter. Going back to our roots often helps remind us of why we love our friends in the first place. A lot of things can get messy along the path of a friendship. Tension, separation, distance, among other things can make our friendships fuzzy and hard to understand. When you retrace your friendship far back enough, you'll eventually rediscover the foundation of your friendship.

It's a humbling thought, but our time on this earth is limited. We don't know how many days we each have left, which makes each day a treasure. What I learned from Reagan and I learned about Jesus is - don't hold back with your friends. Life is too short to be idle with them. Be wild, be crazy, be fun, go on spontaneous road trips, show them parts of your personality that you're afraid to show, do things that are out of your comfort zone, be kind, be joyful, and love like you're made of sunshine.

"As iron sharpens iron, so one friend sharpens another." Looking at the visual of this verse, the verse speaks of how one metal sharpens another when struck together, but what's hidden is what happens when iron steel is struck together. When it's struck together, the iron is heated past its ignition point and produces a brilliant spark. Iron is even mixed with other chemicals in some fireworks to produce sparkles, glow, flashes, and color.

Imagine if we had this power to produce that kind of spark in our friends. We could make them glow and flash with intense color. Now get this: we do have that power. All it takes is that initial encounter and blaze of joy that will ignite the flame. But you have to be willing to be wild and fearless to run full speed into that relationship. You can't hold back; you can't think twice about hopping on for a motorcycle ride. You may even have to reveal all of yourself along the way. It's scary, no doubt, but being vulnerable will be well worth it in the end. Be that wild friend, come unhinged with them, grab some pasta, and throw it down their shirt! I guarantee you'll get a lot more than a dirty shirt.

EPILOGUE

My friends have taught me a lot and shown me how Jesus teaches us to be friends. As you've seen, friends can be a lot of things, but Jesus is everything. This is how we were meant to live our life: sharpening each other and forging relationships through vibrant love.

Friendships aren't always perfect. We all screw up. In order to know each other deeply, we have to be honest with one another and love without ceasing. My friends have sharpened me, and that sharpness is not meant to be idle. It's meant to be used to keep sharpening others.

The way friendships last is with Jesus at the center. Without Jesus, we are simply metal waiting to be shaped. He makes us into his ironwork. He is the one that causes the sparks to illuminate with bursts of color when we sharpen each other.

If you're looking to be a good friend, look to Jesus and you'll know how to do it. He is where the friendships are made, people are shaped, and love is created. He is the Ironworks.

PRAYER

When you speak, Lord, I will listen.

I will follow you wherever you lead me.

You tell me to share other's sorrows and bring joy to those who need comfort.

I am not here to be perfect; I am here to blend with my brothers and sisters in the world you designed.

You always have the upper hand, and fears are relinquished through your presence.

I climb mountains, and you are there to be a foothold.

I am exhausted, and you bring new life.

I am lost, and you are there to guide the way.

Even though it may seem like you are in the distance, you are always near, watching over me.

I live to be a servant; I submit to where you want me to be.

In the depths of my sin, you provide grace when I will never deserve it.

You open my eyes to see what is not visible.

I ask you to continue to open my eyes and protect it from the storm clouds that try and mask my vision.

Your hands do what mine could never.

You are just, fair, holy, righteous, and the perfect friend.

Anger is soothed by the teaching of your forgiveness.

Through the past, present, and future, you have changed me
and shown me what life is truly about.
Continue to teach me the love that never fails.
Teach me to be a friend to all.
Teach me to be a friend like you.
Teach me to sharpen others as you sharpen me.
Teach me to be your ironwork.

ACKNOWLEDGMENTS

My friends are the ones who inspired me to write this book, so it's only appropriate to thank them. Without them, this book wouldn't exist. I wouldn't have the fulfilling and adventurous life I do today if I didn't have them as a part of my story. There's many more stories I could tell, some with other friends, and I wish I could write about them all. I am so incredibly thankful to everyone who has had some part in my life and has sharpened me into the person I am today.

That being said, I have a few extra people I'd like to thank for inspiring me to write this book. Although it is impossible to mention them all, there are a handful that stand out:

- Thank you to Elizabeth, who helped perfect my writing in this book.
- Thanks Mom, Dad, Micah, and Blake for loving me through it all.
- Thank you to one of my oldest friends, Emma, who did stellar photography work for my book cover design. Check her out at Emma Reaves Photography. P.S. I'll never forget how you spit strawberry milk all over me through your nose.

- Shout out to The Real Familia (Mikayla, Reagan, Garrett, Naomi, Travis, and Austin). You guys are my lifeblood.
- Shout out to my work friend/boss Theresa for always keeping it real with me.
- kp, for opening the doors to an adventure with Jesus
- Thanks to Chandler, a friend to all.
- Thank you to Nicol and Felix Guzman for harboring me as your fifth son. Thank you to Jeremiah, Jonathan, Jacob, and JT for being my other set of brothers. The years we spent together have had one of the biggest impacts on who I am today. I love you guys.
- Shout out Hali for encouraging me to follow Jesus and for the wild sing-alongs.
- Special thanks to Matt for previously having a really cool houseboat and for being an amazing friend. You get the special thanks because you asked to be acknowledged. Don't worry, you would have been in here regardless.
- Thanks to all my cousins and to the Three Musketeers (Kait & Dak).
- Thanks to my aunts (Peggy, Judy, Betty, Tawana). Your love for me and generosity has always made me feel overwhelmed with gratitude.
- Shout out Uncle Tommy. I really, really tried to find a way to incorporate a lesson into you biting into a raw fish, but I just couldn't.

- On the subject of fish, shout out AJ for being the realest. I also tried to think of a way I could incorporate throwing a fish down your shirt into a lesson, but alas I couldn't.

- Shout out to my Young Life team for loving me and others vibrantly (Shelby, Rachel, Connor, Kayla, Juliet, Madeleine, Zach, Zubair)

- Big thank you to all my froomies. Thank you, Chris, for energizing me with excitement. Thank you, Cody, for knowing my heart so well. Thank you, Jack, for always checking in on my progress with this book and encouraging me to pursue it. Thank you, Brady, for pushing me to keep grinding on this book and for being an amazing friend to all. Anyone lucky to know you will treasure your friendship.

- Again, thank you to everyone who has had a part in supporting, loving, and knowing me throughout my life. Much love to you all.

Made in the USA
Columbia, SC
28 October 2018